BOLIVIA

TITLES IN THE MODERN NATIONS OF THE WORLD SERIES INCLUDE:

Afghanistan	Japan
Argentina	Jordan
Australia	Kenya
Austria	Lebanon
Brazil	Liberia
Cambodia	Nigeria
Canada	North Korea
China	Norway
Congo	Pakistan
Cuba	Peru
Czech Republic	Philippines
Egypt	Poland
England	Russia
Ethiopia	Saudi Arabia
Finland	Scotland
France	Spain
Germany	Sudan
Greece	Sweden
Haiti	Taiwan
Hungary	Thailand
India	Turkey
Iran	United States
Iraq	Vietnam
Ireland	Yemen
Israel	
Italy	

MODERN
NATIONS
—OF THE—
WORLD

BOLIVIA

BY MARGUERITE A. KISTLER

LUCENT
BOOKS®

THOMSON
——★——™
GALE

San Diego • Detroit • New York • San Francisco • Cleveland • New Haven, Conn. • Waterville, Maine • London • Munich

THOMSON
GALE

On cover: La Paz at night, Illimani in the background.

LIBRARY OF CONGRESS CATALOGING-IN-PUBLICATION DATA

Kistler, Marguerite A.
    Bolivia/by Marguerite A. Kistler.
        v. cm. — (Modern nations of the world)
    Summary: Discusses the topography, history, people, and art of Bolivia as well as the
    challenges the country is currently facing.
    Includes bibliographical references and index.
        ISBN 1-59018-531-5 (alk. paper)
        1. Bolivia—History—Juvenile literature. [1. Bolivia] I. Title. II. Series.

CONTENTS

INTRODUCTION

A NATION OF DIVERSITY

The wonderful diversity of the people of Bolivia is a result of their near total isolation for many generations. This lack of foreign influence has served to preserve their distinct cultures. The rugged, snowcapped Andes mountains and the windswept altiplano, or highlands, were uninviting to all but those who, following the tradition of their ancient ancestors, scratched out a life there. The challenging, but beautiful, terrain of the *montaña* and the *yungas*, both part of the eastern foothills of the Andes, were settled by those who fled there for safety, or were sent there by conquerors. The foreboding eastern regions with rain forest and swamps to the north, and deserts with dry, scorching heat to the south, were too remote and full of danger and hardship to appeal to more than a few scattered tribes. As a result, the isolated people of each area had generations to develop and reinforce their individual cultural heritage.

UNITY IN DIVERSITY

Although their cultures developed separately, Bolivians today have much in common. The Bolivian people are described by the nationals of other South American countries as "easygoing." They are not easily provoked and seem generally content in their daily lives. However, this idyllic description is misleading. The history of Bolivia illustrates the fury that results when these "easygoing" people unite against a common enemy. For example, the indigenous Indian tribes of the Inca and the Aymara rose up against the Spanish, with an intensity that made the Spanish realize that their grasp on the colony was not as tight as they had believed. Years later the Criollas (those of Spanish descent who were born in the colonies), the Quechua of Inca descent, and the Aymara were inspired by Simón Bolívar to unite as one group in a revolt against the Spanish. Bolívar's plea was, "Unity, unity, unity—that must ever be our motto. The blood of our citizens is varied: let it be mixed for the sake of unity."[1] The Bolivians united to break the bands of colonization and to become one nation in 1825.

For over one hundred years, trading, wars, and migration brought these ethnic groups together in towns and cities. With all their differences, they again united as the Aymara, the Quechua, the *mestizo* of mixed Spanish and Indian blood, and the Bolivians of Spanish descent fought the Revolution of 1952 against the Bolivian government, which was backed by the military. In the years since the revolution, the divisions between the ethnic groups have become less distinct as cultural lines have become more blended.

BEAUTY IN DIVERSITY

Even with this blending, many examples of cultural heritage are still seen. The native languages, the beautiful clothing, and the music so distinct to each area remain vibrant even today. One still hears the melodic sound of Quechua, the

Despite the political hostilities between them, the Inca and Aymara Indians united to resist the invading Spanish conquistadores in the sixteenth century.

Bolivia's diverse ethnic groups have managed to maintain their unique cultural identities across the centuries. Here, an Aymara girl wears a hat unique to her people.

language of the Inca. The rougher tones of the Aymara language have changed little since pre-Inca times. In the cities and larger villages, more Spanish is heard, with a smattering of words from the other two languages. All three are official languages in Bolivia.

The diversity of Bolivian ethnic groups extends to the special styles of clothing and hats that are worn. The traditional clothing of the Quechua and the Aymara people has remained unchanged for generations and is very distinctive, including skirts and hats specific to each culture or region. The beauty of Bolivian music also greatly varies by region—from whispering woodwinds to pounding drums, displaying the ethnic influences of the area.

CHALLENGES OF DIVERSITY

With a diverse population comes the challenge of meeting the needs of so many different people. The victory in the Revolution of 1952 was a giant leap toward equality and empowerment, but brought few improvements in the basic problems Bolivians face. Although there is a tiny percentage of wealthy people and a growing middle class, Bolivia is predominantly a nation of the poor. The majority of Bolivians earn less than two dollars each day. The rural poor face the most severe poverty. Houses with no plumbing or electricity, malnutrition, and limited health care make their lives a daily struggle.

In the past Bolivia's government has been unable to meet the most basic needs of its people. Recently, however, gains from gas reserves and finances from foreign investors have begun to stabilize the economy. Disagreements over how much development should take place in areas of the rain forest and grasslands divide those who want to produce as much as possible to boost the economy and those who want to preserve the environment. Bolivians are weighing the benefits of production with the losses to the environment in order to meet this challenge.

In spite of their ethnic diversity and the challenges they face, Bolivians are united as a people of perseverance and faith. They overcame conquerors and scraped out an existence in some of the most brutal ecosystems in the world. They banded together in communities and supported each other, long before there was a civil government to turn to. The strength of their faith—a blending of the Catholic religion and the precolonial religions of their ancestors—is seen in their everyday life through worship, traditions, and festivals. Determination and devotion, as well as respect for the traditions of the past, bind the people of Bolivia together as they deal with the present and look toward the future.

1

A Diverse Topography

Bolivia's geography is very diverse and includes a wide range of natural features. Part of the "rooftop of the world," with its snowcapped Andes mountains, Bolivia also gives two-thirds of its area to tropical and semitropical lowlands. It varies from high, dry plateaus with numbing cold winds to tropical rain forests with suffocating heat and humidity. Arid salt flats give way to lush valleys with refreshing waterfalls. Because of these great variations, nearly every possible ecosystem is seen within Bolivia's borders. "Many of the world's climates and ecosystems exist within this one country," suggests author Mark Cramer. "In some places, a short bus ride or a robust hike can take you from one climate to another."[2]

A Landlocked Nation

Situated in South America, Bolivia is encircled by Peru and Chile to the west, by Brazil to the north and east, by Paraguay to the southeast, and by Argentina to the south. Consequently, it is landlocked, having no access to an ocean. With an area of 424,165 square miles, it is roughly the size of Texas and California combined, and is the sixth largest country in South America.

Located in the Southern Hemisphere, Bolivia experiences summer from November to April; these months bring the most precipitation. Winter lasts from May to October. Temperatures generally vary according to the altitude—the higher the elevation, the lower the temperature.

Bolivia's roughly 8.5 million people are scattered throughout four very different geographic regions, spanning from west to east: the Andes mountains, the altiplano, the *yungas* and the *montaña*, and the Oriente.

The Andes Mountains

The Andes mountains stretch for over forty-five hundred miles along the entire length of western South America. Although the Himalayas of Asia are higher, the Andes range is the longest high-mountain range in the world. In Bolivia the Andes break into two ranges, separated by a plateau, which runs roughly north to south.

The western range, called the Cordillera Occidental, has peaks with an average elevation of 16,500 feet. At 21,463 feet, Mount Sajama is the highest peak in the western range and is famous not only for its height, but also for its beautiful snowcapped peaks and the challenge it presents to mountain climbers. Several active volcanoes in this range vent sulfurous gases. Passes are blocked with snow for several months each year, forming an imposing barrier between Chile and Bolivia, and thus making travel between the countries difficult.

The Cordillera Oriental is the broader, more broken eastern range. The many passes between the mountains allow access to the eastern regions of the nation. One of the highest peaks in this range is Illimani, at 21,201 feet above sea level. Considered one of the most beautiful sights in South America, it towers above the capital city of La Paz. Many of the peaks in this range remain snowcapped year-round. Snow is common above sixty-five hundred feet, with a permanent snowline beginning at 15,100 feet. Above eighteen thousand feet a polar climate exists with icy winds and fierce snowstorms. The lowest temperature ever recorded in Bolivia was recorded here at sixty degrees below zero.

Bolivia's national bird, the giant condor, considered to be a messenger of God and a bearer of good luck, makes its home in the Andes mountains. More than four feet high, it has a wingspan of ten feet and builds its nest at elevations of ten thousand to sixteen thousand feet. The vicuña can also be found in these mountains. Similar to the llama and the alpaca, the vicuña is smaller and produces wool that yields a much softer fabric. This fabric was once reserved for Inca royalty. Spanish chronicler Bernabé Cobo described the clothing of the rulers as "made of the finest wool . . . most of it was made of vicuña wool, which is almost as fine as silk."[3]

THE ALTIPLANO

The high plateau between the two mountain ranges extends five hundred miles from north to south. This plateau is called the altiplano, meaning "high plains." Its soil is a mixture of gravel, sand, and clay from the surrounding mountains. The plateau's width is about eighty miles and its average elevation is thirteen thousand feet. The thin air at these altitudes can cause breathing difficulties for those not accustomed to

it. Altitude sickness, called *soroche*, often results. The symptoms, which include headaches and weakness, can last for a few days until the body adjusts to the lower oxygen density. Since the thin air cannot hold the heat at this high altitude, the temperature falls quickly at night.

Snow-capped Illimani, one of the highest peaks of the Cordillera Oriental, overlooks La Paz, Bolivia's capital city.

On the eastern half of the altiplano there are extensive mineral deposits and fertile soil. The silver deposits found here were nearly exhausted over the three-hundred-year rule of the Spanish. Later, vast amounts of other minerals, including tin and zinc, were discovered. On the western half of the altiplano the soil is not fertile, and there are few mineral deposits. In the southwestern regions lie large salt flats. The Uyuni salt flat covers 4,674 square miles, making it the largest salt flat in the world. The salt deposits can be up to sixteen feet deep. Very little vegetation grows in this environment.

Throughout the altiplano, excluding the salt flat regions, herds of domesticated llama and alpaca graze on the coarse grass called *ichu*. Sheep, brought to the area by the Spanish, thrive here as well. The llama, the alpaca, and the sheep provide meat and wool. Altiplano residents use llamas as beasts of burden and their dried dung, called *taquia*, in place of wood to make fires.

LAKE TITICACA

Lake Titicaca lies on the northern portion of the altiplano. At an elevation of 12,500 feet, it is the highest navigable lake in

Mounds of salt cover the Uyuni salt flats, the world's largest salt flat, located in the southwestern region of Bolivia.

the world. Peru claims the western shore, while the eastern shore belongs to Bolivia. According to author Deanna Swaney, "Lake Titicaca is an incongruous splash of blue amid the parched dreariness of the Altiplano, with clear sapphire-blue waters reminiscent of the Aegean Sea."[4] The Desaguadero River links Lake Titicaca to Lake Poopo, two hundred miles to the south. The great depth of Lake Titicaca sustains much plant and animal life, while Lake Poopo's shallow, salty water cannot.

The land near Lake Titicaca produces root crops, beans, potatoes, alfalfa, and quinoa (a high-protein grain). The people of the altiplano sometimes dehydrate potatoes so that they can be stored and used later. This process involves spreading the potatoes out on the ground, walking on them, and leaving them to dry in the sun. Repeating this each day eventually removes the moisture from the potatoes. The *totora* reed grows on the banks of the lake and can be used to make many items, including fishing boats. These fishing boats last a few months before they become too rotted for use. *Totora* can also be fed to domesticated animals or burned as fuel.

CITIES OF THE ALTIPLANO

Fifty-six miles southeast of Lake Titicaca is La Paz. At twelve thousand feet above sea level, it is the world's highest capital city. Its 1 million people make it Bolivia's largest city, with much cultural, economic, and ethnic diversity. People from all walks of life come together here. As the center of Bolivian commerce and government, La Paz draws both rich and poor, young and old, indigenous and internationals seeking work and a better life. Author Mark Cramer reports:

> It is here where people with nothing but a hope and a prayer converge, entrepreneurs and indigenous Quechuas with only lemons to sell, recent college graduates and highland Aymaras with little formal schooling, international restauranteurs and Cholas, with their bowler hats and wide skirts, who set up sidewalk lunch-stands near construction sites.[5]

On a ridge above La Paz perches El Alto (High Place). Once just a suburb of La Paz, it has exploded into a city of its own, having a population of over five hundred thousand people. Many of these residents commute into La Paz to work as day

At an elevation of 12,500 feet, Lake Titicaca is the highest navigable lake in the world. The lake helps sustain the populations of the northern altiplano.

LAKE TITICACA

The importance of Lake Titicaca to the residents of the northern altiplano cannot be overstated. Historically, Isla del Sol (Island of the Sun), the largest island in the lake, was believed by the Tiwanakan civilization to be the birthplace of both the sun and their leader Viracocha. The Inca also claimed the lake as the birthplace of their civilization. Early inhabitants considered the lake to be bottomless, and it is suggested that the Inca threw vast amounts of silver and gold into the lake during the Spanish conquest. The lake, more than seven hundred feet deep, is also rumored to hold the ruins of an ancient city.

However, perhaps the greatest significance of the lake is the manner in which it influences the nearby climate, as suggested by Herbert S. Klein in *Bolivia: The Evolution of a Multi-Ethnic Society:*

> With its 3,500 square miles, Lake Titicaca exerts an enormous influence over the local climate and provides humidity and relative warmth unavailable on the rest of the altiplano. As a result, intensive agriculture and herding became essential occupations of the peoples surrounding the lake and provided the ecological support for the creation of an important food surplus. This in turn provided the incentive for the creation of more complex cultural systems.

> As in the past, Lake Titicaca continues to nourish the nearby population. Not only can crops be grown here that cannot be cultivated elsewhere on the altiplano, but the lake also provides water for irrigation of otherwise useless land, and is a seemingly limitless source of fish for the residents of the northern altiplano.

laborers, as street vendors, or in private homes. An international airport, which serves La Paz and the northern altiplano, is located here.

The town of Oruro, about one hundred miles southeast of La Paz, has a population of over two hundred thousand people. Once a prominent silver town, it has become a processing center for tin mining and serves as a railroad link to other cities. It is the home of Llallagua, the largest tin mine in Bolivia. Flocks of flamingos gather in the shallow water of Lake Uru Uru south of the city. Oruro has become famous for its folk festivals, which combine music, dancing, and colorful parades.

Southeast of Oruro lies the city of Potosí, with a population of 160,000. At an elevation of 13,700 feet, it claims the distinction of being the world's highest city. This important mining center produces tin, copper, and lead. However, Potosí may be best known for the silver discovered on the nearby Cerro Rico (Rich Hill) in 1544. By 1650, Potosí ranked as the largest and wealthiest city in the Western Hemisphere, shipping tons of silver back to Spain. One legacy of those silver mining days remains: the Casa Real de la Moneda (Royal Mint). It is internationally recognized as one of South America's finest museums. Its old coin-minting machines and its collection of priceless old coins make it a unique treasure.

Near Potosí are hot springs enjoyed by generations of Bolivians. One of these hot springs, Ojo del Inca, is a beautiful green lake in a volcanic crater. It maintains a constant temperature of eighty-six degrees.

THE YUNGAS AND THE *MONTAÑA*

To the east of the Cordillera Oriental range lie two areas of foothills called the *yungas* in the north and the *montaña* in

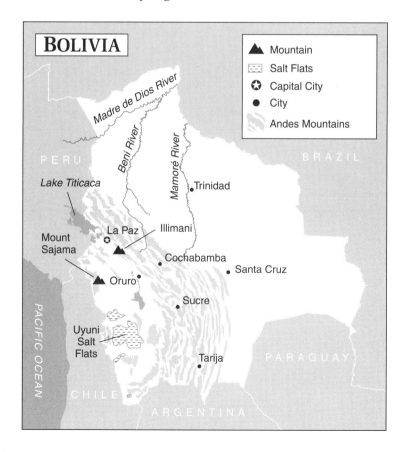

the south. Nicknamed the *ceja*, or "eyebrow," of the mountains, these steep hills and deep valleys have elevations of thirty-nine hundred to eighty-five hundred feet. The *yungas*, from an Aymara word meaning "warm valleys," display rugged, deep chasms and waterfalls. This area receives more rainfall than the *montaña*. In describing the *yungas*, editor Rex A. Hudson says, "The steep, almost inaccessible slopes and peaks of this mainly semi-tropical valley area northeast of La Paz offer some of the most spectacular scenery in Bolivia."[6]

Throughout the *yungas* and the *montaña*, thick, green growth covers the slopes, and the valleys have very fertile soil. Grains and fruits are grown here, along with coca, which is a stimulant that is chewed or used in tea. Coca can also be used in the production of cocaine. Coffee, cedar, mahogany, walnut, and cinchona trees flourish here too. The bark of the cinchona tree yields the ingredients for quinine, which can be used to fight malaria.

Bolivian men harvest coca, a powerful stimulant, on the steep slopes of the foothills of the north known as the yungas.

Jaguars, deer, monkeys, tayras (large weasels), and spectacled bears make their homes in the *yungas* and the *montaña*. The variations in color on the chests, necks, and around the eyes of spectacled bears give them the appearance of wearing glasses. Opposums and armadillos also live in this region.

Cities of the *Montaña*

Roughly in the center of the *yungas* and the *montaña* region is the city of Cochabamba. It is Bolivia's third-largest city, with a population of over six hundred thousand people. Its name means "swampy plains." Cool nights and sunny days give Cochabamba the most pleasant climate in all of Bolivia. Fertile farmland surrounds the city, and factories process the fruits and vegetables grown nearby. Cochabamba has become a trading center for grain and for Peruvian bark, an important ingredient in some medicines. The manufacture of clothing, leather, soap, refined petroleum, and pottery also takes place here.

The city of Sucre, 130 miles southeast of Cochabamba, has a population of nearly two hundred thousand people. Surrounded by high hills, it enjoys a mild, springlike climate. Chosen as Bolivia's capital in 1839, it now holds only the Supreme Court, while the other branches of the government govern from La Paz. Considered by most Bolivians as the nation's prettiest city, Sucre displays many beautiful churches and retains much of its colonial architecture.

At the far south of the *montaña* lies Tarija, Bolivia's lowest and warmest *montaña* city. Although the winter nights are cool, most days are clear and sunny—the perfect climate for producing grapes; this region is well-known for its wine production. Prehistoric fossils are found nearby in the *quebradas* (ravines) and badlands, making Tarija a popular destination for both professional and amateur paleontologists.

The final two-thirds of Bolivia, to the east of the *yungas* and the *montaña*, form a region called the Oriente. These lowlands, with an elevation of only three hundred to fifteen hundred feet, vary in climate, population distribution, and natural resources. The Oriente can be roughly divided into three regions: the rain forest, the farmlands and grasslands, and the Chaco.

THE RAIN FOREST

The northern Oriente, covered by rain forests, is an area of high humidity, high temperatures, and heavy rainfall. As a result, the rain forest supports plant life that could not exist in drier areas, such as rubber trees, brazil nuts, and tropical hardwoods. This lowland tropical forest also provides the perfect habitat for an extraordinary variety of animals, including anteaters, maned wolves, sloths, lizards, spider monkeys, ocelots, and capybaras (the world's largest rodents), as well as many species of birds and insects. River dolphins, otters, alligators, and piranha live in and around this region's slow-moving rivers.

The largest rivers in the rain forest region—the Madre de Dios, the Beni, and the Mamoré—all flow to the northeast, and eventually join the Amazon River. The primary mode of transportation throughout this area is by boat on these waterways.

A small number of Indians from the Guarani and Chiquito tribes live in simple huts in the rain forest of Bolivia. In addition, a few settlers and visiting scientists populate this area. Author Mark Cramer explains that scientists come to this region because of the amazing diversity of natural resources found here: "Bolivia's tropical lowlands are a haven for people whose professions end with 'ologist.' You'll find ecologists, ethnologists, archaeologists, ornithologists, herbologists, and maybe even a tapirologist or a jaguarologist."[7]

Located near the Mamoré River, the city of Trinidad is considered the gateway to the rain forest, as most tours and voyages into Bolivia's rain forest region begin here. Founded in 1556 as an outpost from which to control the indigenous lowland population, nearly eighty thousand people now live in this hot, humid town.

THE FARMLANDS AND THE GRASSLANDS

South of the rain forest and just east of the *montaña* lie the fertile, tropical plains of the farmlands. Although this region receives less rain than the rain forest, it gets enough to sustain corn, vanilla, fruit, rice, tobacco, soybeans, sugarcane, and cotton. With the establishment of large plantations in recent years, there has been a great increase in agricultural production in this region. This increase has created a need for mills to process leather, manufacture lumber, produce textiles, and refine sugar. The farmlands region also contains oil fields, gas fields, and refineries. These fields account for 75 percent of Bolivia's oil and 65 percent of its gas production.

The grasslands stretch from the eastern edge of the farmlands to the border of Brazil. With insufficient rainfall to support the tropical crops seen in the farmlands, this area is devoted mainly to cattle ranching and mining. Beneath the grasslands lie important minerals such as gold and iron.

The largest city in this region is Santa Cruz. As the fastest-growing city in the nation, and with a population of nearly 1 million people, Santa Cruz will soon surpass La Paz as Bolivia's largest city. Santa Cruz also boasts of being Bolivia's wealthiest and most progressive city. Highways and railways link Santa Cruz to other cities and countries, making it a center for trade, transportation, and economic growth. The Santa Cruz area enjoys a very diverse population. It is home to Mennonite farmers, drug traffickers, missionaries, highland immigrants, and Japanese rice farmers.

THE RAIN FOREST

The Bolivian rain forest is both a beautiful and a fearful place. In his 1931 book *Green Hell*, Julian Duguid described the rain forest as "evil, swampy, miasmic, like a warm festering wound." But two pages later he described its beauty as an elegantly dressed woman. "Her dress is magnificent, a rich, eternal garment of every shade of green dappled with gold sun-spots."

These feelings of both amazement and dread are also created by the animal life native to the rain forest. The beauty of a delicate morpho butterfly with its iridescent blue wings inspires wonder, while the sight of the red glow of a caiman's eyes at the water's surface just after dark induces fear. Paradise tanager birds with their squeaky calls compete with the snarls and growls of the jaguar. The delightful sight of a river otter playing in the water is quickly forgotten when one sees a feeding frenzy of the carnivorous piranha. This dense tropical forest, with its extraordinary plant and animal life, is both inviting and intimidating, making it one of the most fascinating places on Earth.

THE CHACO

Finally, the southernmost region of the Oriente, called the Chaco, suffers from one of the most extreme climates in Bolivia. From January to March the weather is hot, humid, and rainy, turning the plains into swamps. Conversely, from April to December the days remain hot, but with hardly any precipitation. The Chaco holds the record for the hottest temperature ever recorded in Bolivia—at 115°.

Sandy plains and scrub forests cover this area, along with coarse grass and cacti. There are also trees called *quebracho*, or "brake-axe" trees, known for their unusually dense wood. This timber, too heavy to float, is one of the Chaco's main exports. Some cattle ranching takes place here, as well as oil and gas production.

Bolivia's extreme topography has limited its ability to make the best use of its great natural resources. The moun-

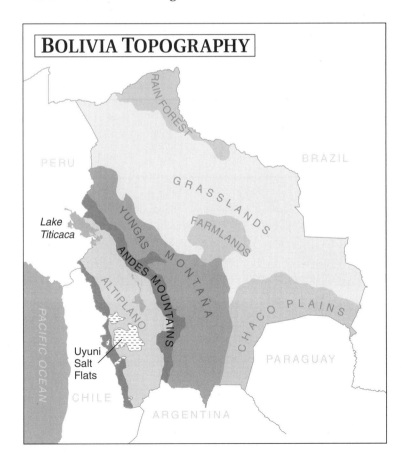

AMBORO NATIONAL PARK

Just a three-hour drive northwest of Santa Cruz is Amboro National Park. Its great value lies in the fact that it occupies over 1 million acres at the intersection of three different ecosystems. As a result visitors can see wildlife of the rain forest, the *montaña*, and the Chaco in the park. Spectacled bear, jaguar, capybaras, tapirs, river otters, peccaries, and howler monkeys can be seen in their natural habitat here.

Amboro is also known for its multitude of plant and bird species. Seven hundred species of birds have been cataloged, with half of the park still to be explored. The unicorn bird (blue-horned curassow), toucan, and macaw all make their homes here. Six hundred plant species—from bamboo to orchids—add to the beauty of this natural treasure.

tains to the west, the steep foothills in the center, and the daunting regions of the east, all present formidable challenges. It is commonly believed that Bolivia's future lies in the Oriente became of the vast cultivatable land, the relative ease of transportation (when compared to the Andes, the *yungas*, and the *montaña*), and the valuable resources of natural gas and oil located there. However, in order to forecast Bolivia's future, one must first understand its past.

2

INVASIONS AND INDEPENDENCE

For centuries the Andean, Tiwanakan, and Aymara peoples lived in the area now known as Bolivia. These ancient Bolivian cultures gave way to dominance, first by the Inca, and then by the Spanish. With each invasion, oppression fell on the indigenous population, causing changes in their daily lives and traditions. Frustration and anger with the invaders boiled below the surface until it finally found its release in revolution and independence.

PRE-INCAN CULTURES

Humans may have lived in Bolivia, in small scattered groups, as long ago as 7500 B.C. Evidence of permanent settlements with a common government dating from 1500 B.C. has been found on the eastern slopes of the Andes. Around 400 B.C. the Andeans, those who had settled in the Andes, began to spread across the altiplano settling primarily along the shores of Lake Titicaca. Evidence exists of the cultivation of native plants, the use of irrigation to improve the land, the introduction of a freeze-drying method to preserve food, and the domestication of llamas and alpacas. These people developed ways to battle brutal elements in order to survive. Author Maria Rostworowski de Diez Canseco notes, "Andeans succeeded in dominating a harsh environment by joining forces and inventing methods to overcome unfavorable conditions."[8]

From 100 B.C. to A.D. 1000 the Tiwanakan nation rose to power on the shores of Lake Titicaca, apparently absorbing the Andean groups. It established a capital city, Tiwanaku, and expanded by colonizing areas to the east of the altiplano. Soon the highlanders enjoyed the produce of the fertile *yungas* and *montaña* regions, while the eastern regions benefited from the altiplano harvest.

For unknown reasons, the Tiwanakan nation began to decline by A.D. 1000, and by A.D. 1200 had disappeared. It appears that the people scattered, were destroyed, or were assimilated by the Aymara, who were also descendents of the Andean settlers. From 1200 to 1400, small Aymara empires rose up throughout the altiplano. These nations gained strength by banding together. Eventually, the Aymara controlled the entire altiplano. There were between seven and twelve nations in the Aymara kingdom.

The Aymara fortified settlements and expanded the existing trade between the highlands and the foothills to the east, through the *ayllu* system. Extended families shared ownership of land both on the altiplano and in the eastern foothills. Part of the clan lived on the altiplano to oversee the fields and

TIWANAKU STRUCTURES

Tiwanaku was the center of a sun-worshiping kingdom, at the southeastern end of Lake Titicaca. Its ruins give us insight into a culture nearly as advanced as the Egyptian empire at the time of the building of the pyramids.

The largest Tiwanaku structure, called Akapana, resembled a giant pyramid without a point. It measured 650 feet on each of its three sides and was fifty-six feet high. The flat top was large enough to hold buildings and a sunken courtyard. The huge stones used to build the structure fit together without mortar, displaying great architectural skill. In fact, the stonework was so exceptional that the Inca recruited stonemasons from Tiwanaku to build Cuzco centuries later.

Another structure, the Puerta del Sol (Gateway of the Sun), with an estimated weight of ten tons, is carved from a single piece of stone and features a carved figure called the "Portal God," which is surrounded by other intricately carved beings. These works display the highly developed skills of the Tiwanakan nation.

The Puerta del Sol monument of the ancient Tiwanakan people is carved from a single piece of stone.

herds while the rest cultivated the *yungas* and the *montaña.* Author Herbert S. Klein explains, "Each *ayllu* and each nation and its nobility had colonists farming the temperate and semi-tropical valleys. In exchange for highland meats, potatoes, quinoa, and woolen products, these colonists paid with . . . corn, coca, and fruits from the *yungas.*"[9]

INCA INVASION

In the mid-fifteenth century, the Inca nation, based in Cuzco, in what is now Peru, began moving south and east. By 1460 they extended their influence over the western Aymara kingdoms. Appealing to the lords of each region for loyalty, the Inca bribed the Aymara with gifts and promises of rewards such as food, clothing, workers, and women. They also offered to release the indigenous people from work temporarily. This system of rewards, called reciprocity, was described by Juan de Betanzos, a Spanish chronicler who was one of the first to transcribe Inca oral history. He said of the Inca ruler Yupanqui, "To those who rendered services to him,

LIFE DURING INCA TIMES

Life during the time of the Inca rule, from 1460–1530, was in some ways similar to rural life in Bolivia today. Fathers and sons worked in the fields planting, harvesting, or herding their animals, while mothers and daughters spent their time spinning, weaving, cooking, and taking care of the younger children. But in other ways, life was very different.

Men and boys wore loincloths and tunics (similar to ponchos), while women and girls wrapped themselves in a large piece of cloth, with a belt at the waist and a large pin, called a *tupu*, fastening the cloth in the front. Fathers made sandals for the family, while mothers made the clothing.

A young man was sometimes allowed to choose the girl he wanted to marry, but the Inca ruler had to approve the choice. If the ruler approved, the bride brought gifts to the family of the groom. The couple could be married only if the groom's family felt that the gifts were acceptable.

Only the sons of important men went to school. They were taken to Cuzco for four years to learn the Quechua language, the Inca religion, the use of a quipa (a system using knots on a rope to record information), and Inca history. Some girls were chosen at age ten to be trained to spin, to weave, or to be servants. Those considered most beautiful were given as wives to men who pleased the Inca lords or they were used as a sacrifice to the Inca gods.

he granted favors, giving them clothes and women from his lineage and permitting them to rest on their lands for one year."[10]

After the initial conquest of the western kingdoms, this system of reciprocity continued as a means of insuring loyalty. If opposition did arise, the lords and their people were destroyed. This put fear into the hearts of the nearby settlements, which often surrendered without a fight. By this method the Inca dominated the Aymara kingdom as far east as Cochabamba by 1500.

The Inca claimed ownership of all the lands they conquered. They then divided the land among the Inca and Aymara commoners and the Inca ruler. They also dedicated land to their sun god. As a type of taxation, and since no monetary system existed, the common people worked the lands dedicated to the sun and the Inca ruler. They were able to keep whatever was produced on their own portion of land. The Inca also initiated a system of forced labor called the *mita* system. Each year, on a rotating basis, men from each community were required to work for the Inca empire for a few weeks or even months. They labored in the mines, built roads or bridges, or served in the army. Depending on their skills, the men might also be required to farm, to produce goods, or to transfer goods from one place to another. At any given time, 3 percent of a community's males served time away from their families in this *mita* system. With these men away, other community members were expected to take on their work.

A much more intrusive system, called *mitmaq*, relocated workers and their families to areas where their labor was needed, or where the original population had been annihilated because of resistance to the Inca. In these cases, the Aymara and the Inca alike were removed from their ancestral lands and resettled together. Described by author Magnus Morner as a system of population exchange, the Inca's purpose was "to spread Inca customs and the Quechua language and to strengthen by their presence internal security in far away territories of the empire."[11] The *mitmaq* system greatly affected the Aymara. For example, Aymarans began to break their ancient tradition of marrying only within one's community, as young men chose Aymara wives from other communities.

The religious beliefs of the Inca centered around worship of the sun (pictured) and involved human and animal sacrifice.

The religious beliefs of the Inca, whose worship of the sun, ancestors, and the Inca ruler involved human and animal sacrifice, were imposed on the indigenous people. When an Inca ruler died, his body was mummified and then cared for as if he were alive. The ruler's family carried the body with them to special celebrations. The Inca required the indigenous people to recognize the superiority of the Inca gods, but the conquered people had the freedom to worship their own gods as well.

The Aymara resented the Inca and the restrictions placed upon them. They resisted the use of the Inca language, called Quechua, continuing to speak the Aymara language and their local dialects. Even more hated was the possibility that their sons and daughters might be among those periodically sent to Cuzco to serve the Inca nobility. Although there were attempted uprisings by the Aymara, including a revolt in 1470, they were quickly and brutally put down.

DEVELOPMENT UNDER INCA RULE

With the Inca conquest came some significant advances, perhaps the most important being the network of roads built during their rule. An estimated fourteen thousand miles of routes, many following ancient trails, connected even the farthest points of the kingdom. Huts or houses, built at set distances along the way, housed runners ready to carry messages or special items throughout the empire. Using this relay system, messages could be taken 150 miles each day. Inns, called *tambos*, and small groups of houses were constructed along the roads to house travelers. This road system

Ruins of an Inca fortress sit above terraced fields in Peru. The Inca introduced terraced farming to Bolivia.

also made it feasible to deliver food and other products to all regions of the kingdom.

A second improvement involved terracing the land to increase the amount of crops that could be grown. This was accomplished by leveling steep hillsides into many tiers, like the seating in a stadium. These tiers held more rainfall and provided more surface area for planting. This terraced farming allowed crops to grow on many acres of land that were previously unusable.

As a result of the abundance of produce, and the need to stockpile items for the widespread kingdom, the Inca constructed warehouses along the network of roads. They designed and situated the warehouses so that proper ventilation prevented spoilage. Dehydrated meat and fruit, grains, tubers, and coca leaves were stored there.

With Inca domination lasting less than one hundred years, the adoption of the Inca religion, culture, and language failed to take hold. In some cases, the indigenous people combined their religious beliefs with those of the Inca, while in the more remote regions the Inca beliefs had no effect at all. Author

AYMARA TRADITIONS

Many aspects of the ancient Aymara culture are a mystery. With no evidence of written language at the time of the Spanish invasion, only oral traditions and archaeological finds give us insights into their beliefs.

The stories that have survived tell of a warlike people who worshiped the sun and other elements of nature. They believed that condors, panthers, and various other animals were sacred. Viracocha was their name for the creator god; Pachamama, their "Earth Mother," and Khuno, the deity of evil. Sacrifices were made to these gods to secure their blessing or to prevent their anger. Medicine men, called *maestros*, made offerings and prayed to the gods (often in song), and healed sicknesses with natural medicines.

Many of the Aymara artifacts and sculptures were confiscated or destroyed by the Inca and the Spanish invaders. However, archaeologists have found carvings of human-like figures, which may represent their gods. Other carvings of plants and animals have also been found. Each discovery gives a small glimpse into this ancient culture.

Maria Rostworowski de Diez Canseco states, "When the *mitmaq* left for distant lands, they carried their idols with them. The humble people turned to their own *huacas* [idols of gods] when in need and not to the Sun of the Incas who probably filled them with dread."[12]

SPANISH INVASION

In the sixteenth century the Aymara and the Inca faced a powerful invader. In 1532 Spanish conquistadores in search of gold and silver made contact with the indigenous people of what is now known as Peru. Leaders Francisco Pizarro and Diego de Almagro arrived on the Pacific coast with 170 conquistadores and began to move inland, claiming the land for Spain and subduing the people as they went.

The Spanish conquest was facilitated by two factors. The Inca empire had just gone through a civil war in which two brothers fought for the throne. This divided the Inca kingdom, making it weak and vulnerable. The hostility of the Aymara people toward the Inca also worked in the conquistadores' favor. Rostworowski suggests that for the Aymara, the years of Inca rule "had not erased the memory of their past liberty, and the majority of the great Andean lords were only waiting for the opportunity to shake off the Inca presence."[13] To the Aymara, the Spanish offered themselves as liberators from the Inca.

The military superiority of the Spanish made the ensuing battles extremely one-sided, in spite of fierce resistance by various indigenous groups. The use of horses, cannons, and guns assured the Spanish victory even though they were greatly outnumbered. The Spanish eventually captured and imprisoned the Inca leader, Atahuallpa. The Inca paid a huge ransom estimated at 13,420 pounds of gold and 26,000 pounds of silver; in spite of this, Atahuallpa was executed. The Spanish conquistadores continued to march inland until 1538, when the area that is now known as Bolivia was claimed for Spain and named "Upper Peru."

RICHES AND RELIGION

Spain's two main purposes for colonizing South America were to increase its wealth and power, and to bring Christianity to the Inca and Aymara. After the defeat of the Inca empire, the Spanish began to carry out these missions, and over the next three hundred years they drastically changed the lives of the indigenous peoples.

In order to teach Christianity to the people, the Spanish built churches in various regions and brought in priests. They discouraged, but tolerated, most of the indigenous religious beliefs and rituals with the exception of the preservation of the mummified remains of important Inca ancestors. The Spanish destroyed these mummies in an attempt to stamp out what they saw as the worship of the dead.

The Spaniards quickly gained power over the Indians by using the indigenous population as laborers. Francisco Pizarro divided the large tracts of land among the conquistadores who had fought with him. The Spanish government also gave the conquistadores the right to use the nearby Indians for labor in exchange for meeting their basic needs and teaching them about Christianity, both of which were accomplished. Unfortunately, the divisions of these large estates broke up many communities and family groups.

To better control the collection of tributes, or taxes, Spain implemented a relocation program. As the Spanish established towns at important points along the roads and around agricultural centers, indigenous people were removed from their native lands and forced into these towns. Called *reduccion*, this was a serious blow to the important indigenous tradition of remaining on ancestral lands.

In 1545, one year after silver was discovered on Cerro Rico (Rich Hill) in what is now Potosí, the Spanish advanced their goal of wealth by claiming possession of any "sub-surface resources." The mines of Cerro Rico became the most productive silver mines ever discovered in the Western Hemisphere. In the first thirty years of production, over 1.5 billion dollars worth of silver was shipped to Spain. Potosí produced nearly twenty-five thousand tons of silver over the course of Spain's three-hundred-year rule. As a result of the flood of workers and people in quest of riches, the town of Potosí soon grew to over one hundred thousand people.

In order to increase food production to meet the demands of these growing towns and villages, the Spanish introduced the use of simple tools unknown to the indigenous people. The iron foot plow, which resembles a spade, helped in cultivating the rocky, steep slopes, while the ox-drawn plow im-

Although Inca leader Atahuallpa converted to Christianity to save himself from burning at the stake, the Spanish conquistadores still executed him.

proved the efficiency of farming on larger, flat tracts of land. When they longed for foods from their homeland, the Spanish also brought sheep, pigs, and chickens to the colonies. Barley, beans, and wheat were planted alongside the native quinoa.

SEEDS OF REVOLUTION

From the beginning of the Spanish domination, rebellions sprang up throughout what had been the Inca empire. Manco Inca, half-brother of the slain Inca ruler Atahuallpa, had been set up as a "puppet" king by the Spanish, a powerless position meant to give the indigenous people the feeling that little had changed. But Manco Inca was not content with this role, and in 1536 he gathered together an army to attack the Spanish in Cuzco. After his defeat, other rebellions arose, each subdued by the Spanish. To overcome the eastern lowland peoples, the Spanish systematically annihilated the most troublesome tribes.

In the 1570s, Francisco Toledo, the viceroy of Lima, Peru, was sent by the Spanish government to Upper Peru to deal with the colony's economic and social concerns. He continued the system of *reduccion*, in which over 129,000 Indians in nine hundred villages were removed from their ancestral lands and gathered in forty-four towns. Although the Indians rebelled against this system, thousands of them were forcibly relocated. Over the next two hundred years, dozens of their revolts were crushed by the Spanish.

During the 1770s and 1780s, Tupac Amaru rose as a leader in the rebellions against the Spanish. He was an important Indian chief who was chosen by the Spanish government to be an official representative of the Indian people. After he failed in a legal attempt to abolish the *mita* system, he began to gather Indian leaders to overthrow the Spanish. Author Herbert S. Klein states, "He was able to convince the overwhelming majority of the Quechua and Aymara *kurakas* [leaders] that Spanish rule had to be destroyed."[14] In spite of fierce fighting on the part of the Indians, by 1783 the Spanish crushed all the major revolts and an uneasy calm prevailed. However, the discontent of the conquered people continued to grow.

They were especially angered by the expansion of the *mita* system. The Spanish continued the *mita* system instituted by the Inca, but increased the number of men sent from each community from 3 percent to nearly 14 percent of the male population. Many of these men worked in the silver mines, and thousands died each year from the dangerous conditions both above and below the ground.

At the same time the Spanish citizens born in South America, called Criollas (or Creoles), resented being excluded from leadership positions in the colonial government. Instead, men from Spain who possessed little knowledge of the culture, politics, or customs of the people filled the most important positions. This resulted in much bitterness as the Criollas began to think of their territory less as a colony that belonged to Spain, and more as a country that belonged to them.

As other nations began to step away from monarchies and become independent, the possibility of independence became more real to those in the Spanish colonies. The United States seized its independence from Britain, and France overthrew its monarch. And with Spain's government weakened by the Napoleonic Wars in which the emperor of France placed his brother Joseph on the throne of Spain, the colonists felt that the time was right to begin their fight for independence.

REVOLUTION

On July 16, 1809, a revolt marked the beginning of the long fight for independence. In the city of La Paz, Pedro Domingo Murillo, a Criolla rebel, led a rebellion with a small group of followers and proclaimed the independence of Upper Peru (now known as Bolivia). This began the South American Wars of Independence. However, the La Paz revolutionaries had moved too quickly and had only one thousand men to fight the five thousand Spanish soldiers sent against them. Other cities joined in the revolution, but by November, Murillo and his followers suffered execution or exile. Herbert S. Klein notes, "Having been the first region formally to declare for independence, Upper Peru [Bolivia] would paradoxically become the last region in South America to gain it."[15] As the fight for independence developed, the revolutionary leaders finally succeeded in uniting the Criollas, the Quechua, and the Aymara to fight Spain.

One of these leaders was Simón Bolívar. Born into one of the oldest and richest families in South America, Bolívar chafed under the rule of Spain. He was allowed to own property, but he could not hold any high office in the government. His family was heavily taxed for any trade it did. With strict regulations on trade, on the purchase of books, and on where one could travel, he and the other colonists were under the control of a government half a world away, in which they had no voice. Bolívar began to take the lead in the fight for freedom. Under his leadership, and the leadership of others like him, the colonists battled across the lands that would become Peru, Argentina, Chile, Ecuador, and Bolivia. As they gathered support for their cause, they gained control of the rural areas, while the Spanish continued to hold the cities. With the Spanish forces divided across such a large area, they

Simón Bolívar helped lead the colonies of South America to independence from Spain. Upper Peru became the independent nation of Bolivia in 1825.

eventually weakened. The revolutionaries began to defeat the Spanish army, and one by one the other South American colonies declared their independence.

The fight for Upper Peru revived again in 1823 when Bolívar's army, led by Andrés de Santa Cruz, a former Spanish officer turned revolutionary, captured La Paz and Oruro. Other rebels captured Cochabamba. In December of 1824, the fighting culminated with the Battle of Ayacucho. At the peak

of the battle, the Spanish forces, led by Viceroy José de la Serna, believed they were on the verge of victory. The Spanish soldiers were ordered to advance quickly to divide the colonists, led by General Antonio José de Sucre. Instead, the Spanish forces split and the colonial cavalry swept down on them and captured the viceroy, forcing surrender. After nearly sixteen years of conflict throughout South America, the Battle of Ayacucho brought the end of Spain's three-hundred-year domination. For his statesmanship and military leadership in the struggle, Bolívar earned the titles "The George Washington of South America" and "El Libertador" (The Liberator). On August 6, 1825, Upper Peru became the separate, independent nation of Bolivia.

3

THE CHALLENGES OF INDEPENDENCE

Gaining independence did not solve the many problems of Bolivia. Chaos, greed, and wars have plagued this struggling nation from its beginning. The physical and economic destruction caused by the war forced the new nation to face nearly insurmountable challenges. Editor Rex A. Hudson states, "The wars of independence had disrupted the economy, the entire mining industry was in decline. Agricultural production was low . . . the government had serious financial difficulties because of huge military expenditures."[16] Before the nation could move ahead, it was forced to deal with the tremendous damage left by the Wars of Independence.

INITIAL CHALLENGES AND REFORMS

Immediate challenges after the war for independence included dealing with the economic realities of the destruction of mining and agriculture. In the mining sector, mines were flooded or collapsed. The few tools and pieces of equipment used before the war were missing or destroyed. After the devastation of the mining operations, nearly half of the ore mined was gathered from the rubble already taken out of the mines. Miners searched slag heaps for any remaining silver that could be salvaged.

The extensive damage to agriculture left barely enough food for the people of the nation. Bolivians had not been able to plant or tend their fields during the past year. The destruction and use of surplus crops left storehouses empty. Limited and destroyed transportation systems crippled Bolivia's ability to move crops throughout the country.

As the people struggled with these stark realities, Bolívar, chosen as first president of the new nation, set about to enact many significant reforms. He began by proclaiming the equality of all Bolivians, reducing tributes by more than one half, and giving the Indians ownership of the lands on which they lived. He wrote Bolivia's constitution, which initiated the abolition of slavery for the thousands of Africans brought to the colony by the Spanish. The constitution also called for freedom of speech, instituted the system of trial by jury, and framed the government as a democratic republic ruled by a president rather than a monarchy ruled by a king.

In 1826 Bolívar was needed to settle disputes in Peru, Colombia, and Venezuela, so he turned the government over to Antonio José de Sucre, the former revolutionary comman-

Revolutionary Antonio José de Sucre served as Bolivia's president from 1826 to 1828.

der, whom he loved like a son. Sucre served in Bolívar's absence and was then elected president in 1826. In one of his attempts to meet the financial needs of the new government, Sucre confiscated much of the wealth of the Catholic Church and sold the property of twenty-eight of the forty Bolivian monasteries. The money this brought to the Bolivian government was not enough to meet the country's needs. Sucre also reinstated the tributes that Bolívar had greatly reduced. These two steps alienated many Bolivians. With former friends turning against him, and after an attempt on his life, Sucre resigned and returned to his home in Venezuela.

Andrés de Santa Cruz led Bolivia from 1829 to 1839, bringing a period of relative stability. He developed important blueprints for the new nation to follow. He greatly increased the mining and textile output by the use of protective tariffs,

MINING IN BOLIVIA

Mining has always been a cold, dirty, tiring, and dangerous job. During the three hundred years of Spanish rule in Bolivia, millions of men died in mining accidents and of diseases spread among the miners, such as silicosis (from inhaling quartz dust) and tuberculosis.

After Bolivia won its independence, only the owners of the mines changed. The workers—generally Indians and former slaves—continued their backbreaking labors. As veins of ore near the surface were depleted, the miners had to go deeper and deeper into the earth. There were no power tools, only candles for light, and nothing to circulate the dust-filled air.

Even today, with mining tools, added safeguards, and health services at the larger mines, miners still deal with tough questions: Should I use my young son or daughter in the mine as a helper? Are these explosives safe? Should I go without buying the helmet, gloves, and steel-toed shoes I need, so I can buy food for my children? Is this persistent cough from tuberculosis, silicosis, or just a cold? In the twenty-first century, mining is still about being cold, dirty, tired—and worried.

which restricted imports from other countries, and reduced taxes, encouraging production within Bolivia. Santa Cruz also instituted a more accurate census. This improved the success of collecting taxes and brought more money to the struggling country. Perhaps most important, Santa Cruz brought ten years of sorely needed peace to Bolivia.

INSTABILITY

However, beginning in 1841, and continuing for nearly 150 years, violence, uprisings, and 190 governmental changes troubled Bolivia. The democratic republic which Bolívar had established was often ruled instead as a military dictatorship by men who ignored the principles of democracy. In November 1830, just a month before his death from tuberculosis, Bolívar wrote to a friend, General Juan José Flores. He feared that the revolution had made little difference and that the best thing to do was to emigrate, or leave the country. Many of Bolívar's sad predictions for the new countries in South America were fulfilled over the next century in Bolivia. Bolívar states:

I have held power for twenty years, and I have drawn but a few sure conclusions: [South] America is ungovernable. The only thing one can do in [South] America is to emigrate. Devoured by all the crimes and extinguished by ferocity, we shall be disdained by the Europeans. If it were possible for a part of the world to fall back to primitive chaos, [South] America would.[17]

Most often it was military leaders, greedy for power or money, who took the nation's leadership by force, suspending democratic elections or ignoring the will of the voters.

Author Deanna Swaney explains, "One military junta after another usurped power from its predecessor, setting a pattern of political strife that would haunt the nation."[18] One president alone, Manuel Isidoro Belzu, had to fight off forty coup attempts in his six years in office. From 1860 to 1880, the Palace of Government became known as the Palacio Quemando, or "Burnt Palace," as it suffered fire damage in one of the many uprisings and violent takeovers of the government.

The most notorious leader of Bolivia during this period, General Mariano Melgarejo, ruled from 1864 to 1870. This military dictator seized the government just before an election was to take place. With no background in politics or economics, he depended on the military's support to rule Bolivia. He confiscated and sold Indian lands using a "confiscation decree," by which Indians were given sixty days to purchase from the government the land on which they lived and farmed. If they could not pay, the land was auctioned off to the highest bidder. Many say that Melgarejo spent vast amounts of the government's money for his personal benefit. One author, Julian Duguid, claimed that, in selling Bolivia's land near Brazil, Melgarejo traded "the entire border in return for a diamond star."[19] Unfortunately, Melgarejo, though considered the worst, was only one in a series of greedy, power-hungry dictators.

ECONOMIC GAINS

In spite of this time of internal unrest, the economy blossomed as the world became increasingly interested in Bolivia's products. New methods and machines, including the steam engine, increased the output of the mines. By 1902 tin was so highly demanded that it surpassed silver as Bolivia's leading export. Bolivia supplied one-fourth of the world's tin by 1918. The increase in profits resulted in higher wages and in the establishment of some schools and health clinics near mining areas.

Further economic gains resulted from the great need for rubber for bicycle and automobile tires. This sparked a boom in the Amazon region of Bolivia, promoting exploration and commerce there. Bolivia's President Mariano Baptista (1892–1896) made the development of this industry a priority, and soon huge amounts of rubber were harvested for export around the world.

A large loan from a private bank in the United States enabled Bolivia to expand its system of railroads, reaching more remote areas and providing the means to move products to markets. Mine owners benefited from this reliable railroad system as it became faster and cheaper to transport ore. Additionally, products could now be shipped from La Paz to both Peru and Argentina. New markets opened for the nation's goods, which brought greater profits in both agriculture and industry.

LANDS LOST

Unfortunately, these years of unprecedented progress were marred as Bolivia lost land to its neighboring countries due to border disputes. Between 1878 and 1883 a controversy over taxation escalated into the War of the Pacific with Chile. Chilean citizens had lived and mined for years in the Pacific coastal region that technically belonged to Bolivia, which allowed the Chileans to do so in exchange for taxes. In 1874 an informal agreement allowed Chile's nitrate companies to escape paying new taxes for twenty-five years in the coastal area of the Atacama Desert. However, the Bolivian government, realizing the value of the region, attempted to impose a new tax in 1878, which the Chileans refused to pay. When Bolivia threatened to seize the company's property, war began and Bolivia lost its only outlet to the Pacific Ocean.

Another simple border dispute resulted in a war, which represents a turning point in Bolivian history. The Chaco border region between Bolivia and Paraguay contained few inhabitants, and its exact borders were not well mapped. In 1932 a dispute developed over this area. Some Bolivians felt that foreign oil companies were behind the conflict as the area was rumored to contain rich oil deposits and both countries had ties to major oil companies. However, author Herbert S. Klein contends that

> Bolivian president Daniel Salamanca pushed the nation into war to shift focus away from his failing economic policies: Salamanca and the Bolivian government deliberately escalated a typical border incident into a full-scale war. It was Salamanca who, against the written

Trucks transport Bolivian draftees from their villages to the front lines of the Chaco War with Paraguay. Bolivia was soundly defeated, losing territory and thousands of lives.

advice of his general staff, forced the conflict beyond any peaceful settlement into what would become Bolivia's most costly war in its republican history.[20]

In the three years of the Chaco War, as it was called, Bolivia lost twenty thousand square miles of land, millions of dollars, and nearly sixty-five thousand men.

UNREST AND REVOLUTION

The Chaco War gave rise to the "Chaco Generation." This term refers to the men who served during the Chaco War, were affected and in many cases disillusioned by what they experienced, and in turn desired changes in their nation. These soldiers began rethinking the rather rigid racial divisions within Bolivia. To this point in Bolivia's history, Criollas generally saw Indians only as servants, and certainly not as equals. But in this conflict the Criollas and Indians served side by side. Social barriers between the groups began to break down as a mutual respect developed. As Klein notes, "The war shattered the traditional belief systems and led to a fundamental rethinking of the nature of Bolivian society."[21]

The Chaco War also reinforced the belief that Indians have the right to participate in the Bolivian political system. Although they were expected to serve, and perhaps die for their country, many Indians had never been allowed to vote. Bolivians had to be able to read in order to vote, and most Indians had no opportunity for formal education. This glaring inequity in their government frustrated the Indians. It also affected their daily lives, since the government leaders, chosen primarily by the Criollas, gave little thought to the needs or desires of the Indians. Instead the leaders made laws and policies to please only those who voted for them.

Political parties and organizations that encompassed all social groups began to form. Author Magnus Morner explains, "The war is a watershed in Bolivia's history. Before, political radicalism had been confined to small groups of intellectuals and union activists. After, embittered war veterans spread radicalism throughout the lower and middle classes."[22] Governmental change resulted, sometimes in nonviolent ways, but more often with great violence. One after another, regimes fell. One of the most violent overthrows occurred in 1946 when Major Gualberto Villarroel, after seizing power, was removed from the Presidental Palace, shot, and hanged in the street.

As tension and unrest increased, the 1951 election became the climax. In that election Victor Paz Estenssoro won the popular vote. His political party, the Movimiento Nacionalista Revolusionario (MNR) favored many labor reforms and promoted both socialist and antigovernment principles. In an attempt to retain power, the military leadership of the government annulled the election and outlawed the MNR party. In response, on April 9, 1952, Estenssoro supporters, miners, and various other groups rose up in revolt in La Paz. In order to defeat the ruling military government, those leading the revolt broke into the stockpile of military weapons and gave them to the general population. The army lacked order as many officers deserted their commands. Only three days after it began, the Bolivian Revolution of 1952 ended and Victor Paz Estenssoro assumed the presidency.

REFORMS AND RELIEF

Some immediate reforms enacted after the revolution affected all Bolivians. A main goal of the new leadership was

Victor Paz Estenssoro (in chair) assumed the presidency after the Bolivian Revolution of 1952, in which Estenssoro overthrew a brutal military dictatorship.

to increase the indigenous people's involvement in Bolivian politics. After the revolution, literacy was no longer a requirement for voting, and all adults were allowed to vote. The number of voters grew from two hundred thousand to almost 1 million.

Prior to the revolution Indians worked their landlord's land for three or four days each week without pay, for the privilege of working a small piece of land for themselves on the other days. Even this small plot belonged to the landowner. After the revolution this form of unpaid labor became illegal

Miners push an ore car into a tin mine. President Estenssoro nationalized Bolivia's three largest tin mines and used the profits to establish schools and health clinics.

and the Indians received ownership of their small pieces of land. However, before this process of breaking up the large estates of land could be put into effect, some Indians seized the land by force. In those cases, the landowners either fled for their lives or were killed.

In another move that benefited Bolivians, Estenssoro nationalized the three largest tin mining companies. Previously they had brought millions of dollars to their owners, but little money or benefits to the workers. Estenssoro bought the mines from their owners and placed them under the government's control. He created COMIBOL (Mining Corporation of Bolivia) to run these state-owned mines. With the profits from these mines, COMIBOL established schools for sixty thousand children, housing for mining families, and health clinics.

Another important reform involved the establishment of elementary schools in all Bolivian communities. This implementation proved a very slow process, but the new government was intent on educating all of Bolivia's children.

After the revolution this struggling nation was greatly aided by foreign countries. The United States sent aid for both humanitarian reasons and to reduce the threat of a communist takeover. Between 1953 and 1960 the United States contributed an average $20 million each year to help stabilize the Bolivian economy and to meet the needs of its people. In 1953 alone, the United States sent food worth a total of $5 million. The International Monetary Fund (IMF), an agency of the United Nations that gives loans and aid to struggling countries, sent resources with the provision that Bolivia must stabilize its economy.

MILITARY REGIMES

The twelve years following the Revolution of 1952 passed in relative peace. However, the many reforms that looked so promising at first either did not raise most Bolivians' standard of living or were not making a difference quickly enough. Disappointment and dissatisfaction led to another cycle of violent regime changes led by military dictators who ignored the constitution, denied the rights of the people, and silenced those who opposed them, sometimes by murder. Over and over, different military leaders took control, sometimes without much of a fight, but more often with bloodshed.

Making Their Voices Heard

The Bolivian people have a history of banding together to make their voices heard. From the Inca uprisings against the Spanish to the Wars of Independence and the Revolution of 1952, change has often come through violence. But in recent years, methods of nonviolent dissent have gotten the attention of the Bolivian leadership, and have brought about change. In *Culture Shock! Bolivia*, author Mark Cramer explains, "Here is history in action, participatory democracy, ritual confrontation that always ends up with negotiated settlements." He means that when Bolivians act within the legal bounds of a democracy, they often bring attention to a need for change.

In January 1996 this participatory democracy took the form of a demonstration, as more than three hundred female coca growers and workers completed a thirty-day march to La Paz to protest the government-sponsored destruction of coca fields in their area. The march of these mothers with their babies brought much sympathy for their cause and prompted the government to listen to their demands.

Groups and individuals have staged hunger strikes, refusing to eat until they are allowed to speak to those in leadership. Work stoppages (strikes) are often used to get the attention of the government. Newspaper articles and letters to civil authorities spread the word about the concerns of citizens. And one of the most effective ways Bolivians make their voice heard is to vote. In all these ways, Bolivians take their role as citizens very seriously.

The government had little stability, and some of the reforms begun after the revolution were not carried out.

General Luis Garcia Meza took power in a violent coup in 1980. He had financing from drug traffickers, and the former Nazi Gestapo chief, Klaus Barbie, helped silence Meza's opposition. Although Meza was only in power for one year, it was a year marked with arrests, torture, and, in some cases, murder for those who opposed him. Once, when a secret meeting of an opposing political party was discovered, Meza sent in soldiers who killed everyone there. Meza opened the floodgates for drug traffickers, and during his one-year regime, Bolivia's cocaine exports totaled $850 million. After suffering under his human rights violations and having had no democratic elections since 1966, the people of Bolivia were ready to restore democracy.

RELATIVE STABILITY

This move away from military dictatorships and toward more democratic leadership has evolved and strengthened in the years since 1982. At that time, Hernan Siles Zuazo won the first constitutional election in nearly twenty years. For the next two decades, political change came without violence.

In 1985 Victor Paz Estenssoro won the presidency for a third time. Believing a strong economy would strengthen Bolivia's democracy, he instituted tough reforms to curb runaway inflation. With inflation at an incredible 24,000 percent, a box of cereal that cost one dollar on January first, cost $240 by December 31. Budgets were frozen, twenty thousand of the twenty-seven thousand mining workers were laid off, and mines were closed down for months to study which ones should open up again. Economic conditions improved, and within months inflation was down to 10 to 20 percent. In an attempt to infuse the economy with new money, the government opened nationalized companies to foreign investors. Relations with other nations improved as Bolivia addressed its problems and instituted more free-market policies.

With Gonzalo Sánchez de Lozada's election in 1993, Bolivia gained a president who sought to institute major reforms in not only the economy, but also in the government and in education. In 1994 he passed the Law of Capitalization, which initiated the sale of the government-owned railroads, airlines, telecommunications, and electricity to private investors. A part of the proceeds from these sales went directly to alleviate poverty. Another reform, the Law of Popular Participation, funneled financial resources to local governments and gave rural towns greater power in deciding how this money should be used. During Sánchez de Lozada's term, constitutional amendments were passed that lowered the voting age from twenty-one to eighteen and extended the term of the president from four to five years. Finally, Sánchez de Lozada enacted educational reforms, which increased bilingual and multicultural instruction, and set up the Human Rights Commission to protect the rights of all Bolivians.

After the five-year term of Hugo Banzer Suárez and his vice president, Jorge Quiroga, Gonzalo Sánchez de Lozada was again elected as Bolivia's president in 2002. His goals were to create jobs by building public housing and a cross-country highway. Health care and an expanded vaccination program were also high priorities as he served Bolivia.

However, on October 17, 2003, President Sánchez de Lozada was forced to resign after weeks of protests resulted in dozens of deaths. The unrest was caused by a proposal to export natural gas to the United States through Chile. While the president estimated that the sale of Bolivia's surplus natural gas would bring millions of dollars to Bolivia each year, those protesting felt that only the wealthy would benefit from the plan. In accordance with Bolivia's

Residents of La Paz congratulate Carlos Mesa after he is inaugurated as president in 2003. Vice President Mesa assumed the presidency after President Sánchez de Lozada resigned.

THE GOVERNMENT OF BOLIVIA

In a system of government similar to the United States, Bolivia's federal government has three branches. The Executive Branch meets in La Paz and is made up of the president, the vice president, and the cabinet, with its fourteen ministers. The president and vice president are elected for a five-year term, while the members of the Cabinet are appointed by the president.

The elected members of the Chamber of Deputies and the Chamber of Senators, which make up the National Congress, serve five-year terms. There are 130 deputies and twenty-seven senators, three from each of the nine departments (departments are similar to states in the United States). These Chambers meet in La Paz.

The Supreme Court of Justice of the Nation makes up the Judicial Branch of the government and meets in Sucre. Its twelve judges are appointed by the National Congress and serve ten-year terms.

constitution Vice President Carlos Mesa stepped in as president.

The most recent presidents of Bolivia have encouraged democratic principles and have strengthened Bolivia's ties with the United States and with its neighboring South American countries. Unfortunately, mounting unrest and political divisions threaten the country's peace and stability, bringing Bolivia to a critical point in its history.

4

DAILY LIFE IN BOLIVIA

Bolivia displays a tapestry of ethnic groups which have remained quite distinct over the years. "Bolivia's distinctive topography and ecology have had an enduring impact on the country's diverse groups," says editor Rex A. Hudson. "The isolation most communities and regions faced until at least the 1950s contributed to cultural diversity."[23] One of the most fascinating aspects of Bolivia is its rich cultural variety. Bolivia contains the largest Indian population of all of the South American countries, with a total of 55 percent, which includes two distinct Indian groups. The Quechua people, of Incan descent, comprise 30 percent of Bolivia's population, while 25 percent claim Aymara lineage as descendants of pre-Inca cultures. The largest ethnic group, called Mestizo, makes up 35 percent of the population and includes those of mixed Indian and Spanish ancestry. Less than 10 percent of Bolivians retain a Spanish heritage. The remainder of the population includes descendants of African slaves, other small indigenous groups in the rain forest, and immigrants from various countries.

Bolivia recognizes three official languages: Spanish, Quechua, and Aymara. Quechua, the language of the Inca, is most often heard in the *montaña* and near Potosí and Oruro. Aymara, the language of the pre-Inca cultures, is spoken around Lake Titicaca and La Paz. People in and around the cities are more likely to speak Spanish. Although 65 percent of the Bolivian population speaks Spanish, it is not the primary language of many of the Quechua and the Aymara.

FAMILY LIFE

In spite of language, cultural, and regional differences, the people of Bolivia have much in common in their daily lives. The basic roles and responsibilities within the family are similar throughout Bolivia. Hudson explains, "A stable family life and widely extended bonds of kinship provide the most effective source of personal security. Although family and kinship practices vary among the disparate ethnic groups, both Hispanic and Indian traditions place great stress upon bonds of responsibility among kins."[24] Families focus on earning a living, caring for each other, and making sure that the children are educated. Both parents help support the family financially. The primary concerns of the women include caring for the home and family and preparing meals. They also sell produce from their fields or fabric they have woven. The men generally work outside the home in the family's fields or in a paid occupation. The children go to school and help by doing chores. At a very young age they take on simple tasks and eventually work to help support the family. With all of this concentration on providing for their families, Bolivians still find ways to celebrate their culture, religion, and family milestones.

RURAL LIFE

About 36 percent of Bolivians live in rural areas, where housing and life in general has changed very little over the past

Quechua and Aymara Indians attend a conference in 2003. Bolivia has the largest Indian population of any South American nation.

two centuries. Most rural houses consist of one story and are made of mud and bricks or stone, with hard-packed dirt floors and thatched, tile, or metal roofs. These houses are sometimes isolated, or may be gathered in small groups. The one or two rooms contain very little furniture other than simple chairs and a table. Families with no beds sleep on animal skins on the dirt floor. Those with a bed sometimes cover its boards with a wool blanket or make a mattress of dried grass. Only 30 percent of rural homes have running water and electricity, and only 3 percent have indoor bathrooms. Any cooking, often done over a fire in a corner, uses sticks or dry llama dung as fuel. Many rural families eat only twice a day—around sunrise and sunset. A simple rural meal might include soup made with potatoes and, on special occasions, perhaps a bit of fish or meat.

Agriculture, herding, mining, weaving, and fishing constitute the main occupations of rural families. Agriculture involves nearly one-half of the population of Bolivia. However,

Rural life in Bolivia has changed very little in the past two centuries. Here, a mother teaches her daughters the ancient craft of blanket weaving.

vast differences exist between Bolivia's farms depending on their size. On small farms, planting and harvesting continues to be done by hand. Fields of grains, potatoes, corn, coffee, coca, or fruit are tended by all but the very young. These small farms produce only enough food to support the family that owns it, called "subsistence" farming. If a surplus of food remains, it may be sold at local markets or to vendors who take the products into the cities. By contrast, larger farms use machinery and many workers to cultivate fields or groves. The flatter eastern regions of Bolivia lend themselves to these larger estates, plantations, and ranches from which most produce is sent throughout the country or exported.

Herding of sheep, alpaca, and llama goes hand in hand with agriculture. Many families that make their living by farming also own a few animals or a herd. These animals yield the wool needed for clothing. Young boys watch over their family's animals, and sometimes care for the animals of other families as well.

At an early age, girls learn to spin wool and to weave cloth. This is important because she will need to supply clothing and blankets for her family, and may one day sell her weavings to help her family financially. Learning these tasks also gives her time to create a special bond with other women of her family and to learn about her culture. "One of the most important aspects of weaving," according to Aymara artist Aymar Ccopacatty, "is the time people spend together. That is when the grandmothers tell the granddaughters about their traditions."[25]

OCCUPATIONS OUTSIDE OF THE HOME

In silver and tin mining areas, the men and boys leave for the mines early in the morning and return as the sun goes down. The young boys and old men work on the lighter tasks, while the young men do the more dangerous or demanding jobs such as blasting and drilling. More recently Bolivians have begun to mine for the "black gold" of the eastern oil and gas fields. This involves exhausting work using heavy equipment. Because of the remote locations of these operations, men sometimes work for a month at a time, and then return home for a month.

Fishing, an important occupation for the men and boys who live near Lake Titicaca or the rivers of the eastern lowlands, provides not only protein and variety in their diets, but also a source of income as they sell their catch in nearby markets or cities. Fishing with nets from small boats remains virtually unchanged from one hundred years ago, although in most cases, wooden boats have replaced the *totora* reed boats once used extensively on Lake Titicaca.

URBAN LIFE

With indoor plumbing and electricity, most houses in the city are not as simple as those in the rural countryside. While over 90 percent of urban homes have running water and electricity, only about half have indoor bathrooms. Houses belonging to the wealthy include all the modern conveniences, while the poor, many who have come to the city looking for a better life, may begin to live in little more than a shack until money can be saved to build something more substantial.

Urban Bolivians enjoy a great variety of foods. They generally eat three times each day, but spend less time preparing meals than their rural counterparts, because of the convenience of stoves and the availability of cooked foods on the streets. Food carts and stands offer everything from cheese-filled pastries to roasted pork. Restaurants prepare kingfish from Lake Titicaca and steak from the Oriente. Fruits and vegetables from across the country are available in the markets. This varied diet more easily meets their nutritional needs than the limited diets of the rural Bolivians.

EARNING A LIVING

Although the basic roles of family members in urban settings generally match those in rural settings, their occupations may differ greatly. Urban women often work as street vendors or maids, or are hired in the city's schools, hospitals, or businesses. Caring for their families takes less time, with easier meal preparation and the option of purchasing rather than making clothes. Men find work as street vendors, shopkeepers, bankers, or in other businesses in the city. Many go into business for themselves, providing products or services that are needed.

Urban children often contribute by running errands or helping with the family business. Some earn money by shining shoes. Shoeshine boys earn about sixty cents a day after

THE SPICE OF LIFE

Food not only meets the daily physical needs of Bolivians, but it is also an important part of their culture. Bolivia's diverse cultures and ecosystems offer a great variety of delicious foods. In the rural areas of the highlands, meals are quite starchy, often including potatoes and corn. If meat is used at all, it is often lamb or guinea pig. In the lowlands more fish, fruit, and rice are eaten. Here armadillo, monkey, or alligator may be used along with the more common beef, chicken, or pork.

At open-air markets in the cities and villages a delicious selection of foods using beef, pork, chicken, lamb, or fish can be found. One favorite choice is the *salteña*, which is a dough shell stuffed with meat, onions, potatoes, peas, black olives, and a bit of hard-boiled egg, all with a spicy sauce. Empanadas are also popular. Not as spicy as the *salteña*, they are filled with similar ingredients, or with cheese.

For sweet treats, there are *jugos* and *licuados* (fruit juices and shakes), or *api*, which is made from crushed corn, sugar, and cinnamon. On festival days, colorful candies, called *confites*, are sold, which are made by wrapping a sugary mixture around nuts, fruit, or coconut.

paying for food and transportation to and from their homes. Although children are required by law to attend school until they are fourteen, these unsupervised youth are usually ignored by the authorities, as they may be earning an income needed by the family.

Some families, or individual family members, live in the city only when no planting or harvesting is being done in their rural villages. In this way, they are able to earn an income for a few months and then return to their villages when it is time to help with the crops.

EDUCATION

Bolivian people place a high value on education. They see it as a way to improve one's life. Although in more rural areas children often have to miss school to help with the family fields or herds, education remains one of the highest priorities of both the government and the people.

Public education begins at the age of six and continues to the age of fourteen, when schooling becomes optional. With

Bolivians living in the cities earn a living in a variety of occupations. Urban women often work as street vendors, like this clothing vendor in La Paz.

few books and other school supplies in rural schools, lessons often involve having students repeat information over and over, or copy math problems and reading assignments from a chalkboard. In cities, a great percentage of children attend school since they are not needed in the fields or mines. The wealthy usually send their children to private schools. Along with lessons in math, civics, and reading, school days include recess with soccer, basketball, or other games.

Although school is not required after the age of fourteen, some young people continue on to secondary school. Rural families sometimes send their young boys to the closest city to continue their education. These boys either stay with relatives or work for a family in exchange for room and board. Seventeen universities and technical schools, located in the larger cities, serve those who desire a college degree. Business, information technology, engineering, architecture, education, and medicine are among the most sought-after degrees.

FAMILY TRADITIONS AND CELEBRATIONS

Family traditions and celebrations reveal the most enduring customs of the past with fascinating insight into the social and cultural fabric of Bolivia. These celebrations involve more than just the immediate family, extending to many friends and relatives. "People of all classes and ethnic groups focus their deepest loyalties on their small community or neighborhood and a close-knit group of relatives,"[26] editor Rex A. Hudson suggests. As a result, although the celebrations vary greatly depending on the wealth of the family, these gatherings bind families, generations, and communities together.

The choosing of godparents, or *padrinos*, continues as an important tradition in Bolivian society. It takes place most often at an infant's baptism or sometimes at a wedding. Occasionally a godparent is chosen, not from the family, but

TRADITIONAL DRESS OF WOMEN

The traditional clothing of Bolivia can tell a story, if one knows how to "read it." The clothing of the indigenous girls and women tells others where they are from and whether they are married.

A traditional skirt is worn over petticoats or underskirts, which make women look heavier than they really are. The many layers add warmth and give the skirt the shape of a bell. The style and length of the skirt reveals the ethnic background of the woman.

A rectangle of woven fabric is folded to produce a pouch to be carried on a woman's back, and is tied around the neck. It is used to carry everything from vegetables to babies. The patterns and colors of the weaving give a clue as to where it was made and the possible origin of the woman wearing it.

The biggest indication is the hat worn by women. The style of the hat immediately tells if the wearer is Aymara or Quechua. Near Potosí and Oruro, stovepipe hats are common. An Aymara woman usually wears a dark green, brown, or black bowler hat, similar to one an English gentleman might wear. If it is slanted to the side, the girl is single. A Quechua woman would be more likely to wear a hat called a *montera*, which has a wider brim and a flat top. When Bolivian women wear these items, they display pride in their culture.

from important people in the community. In theory, this godparent will help the child by giving him a job or helping him financially.

A child's first haircut, called *rutucha*, usually done when the child is one or two, marks another special occasion. The godparents and other relatives take turns snipping away a bit of hair and pinning gifts of money to the child's clothes. For rural children, this money is often used to purchase a llama or a lamb, which will eventually come under the child's care.

Birthdays are celebrated with a gathering of the extended family. Parties for adults include dancing and a late dinner, with a midnight cutting of the birthday cake. Children enjoy snacks and cake at their parties, but gifts often remain unlabeled and unopened until after the party. As a result, the birthday child often does not know from whom his gifts came.

Marriage is considered the most important event in a Bolivian's life and involves much planning and celebration. Urban weddings generally occur on a Saturday and are followed by a party. In some rural areas a series of events must take place before the wedding. This process sometimes extends over several years, beginning when a couple receives permission from their parents to court one another. Next comes the engagement, and then a number of different ceremonies. There is usually a Catholic wedding ceremony, a feast from the godparents, and an inheritance feast in which the couple is promised their portion of the family assets. A planting ritual symbolizes the beginning of their life together and asks Pachamama (Earth Mother) to bless their union. These traditions signify their pledges to each other, the responsibilities of their families and community to them, and the desire for blessings from God and Pachamama.

RELIGION

The most unifying factor in Bolivian life today is religion. Ninety-five percent of the people claim Catholicism as their religion. While the Aymara and the Inca both worshiped natural elements (the sun, the moon, the Earth Mother), the Spanish brought a very different belief system based on one creator, God. The Catholic priests were not able to convince the people to turn away from the gods of their ancestors. Over the years, the people wove together the beliefs of the indigenous religions and the beliefs of Catholicism. This combination of Catholic and indigenous beliefs, called folk-Catholicism, can be observed throughout Bolivia.

Many traditions and superstitions from the indigenous religions remain. Beliefs linger about the gods and spirits who must be appeased with *cha'llas*, or offerings, of alcohol, coca, cigarettes, or occasionally a llama. Before Bolivians drink a glass of alcohol, they spill a few drops on the ground as an offering to the gods. Similarly, they splash a glass of alcohol over a new car or house. Llama fetuses, which can be purchased in a market, are placed under the foundation of a building to bring good luck or protection to those who live or work there.

Bolivians believe that specific gods and spirits have dominion over certain places and aspects of daily life. Pachamama must especially be given respect as it is believed that she allows food to grow and fields to produce. Ekeko, the

A YEAR'S WORTH OF FESTIVALS

Bolivian festivals are a fascinating mixture of pre-Inca, Inca, and Spanish customs, and are, at the same time, religious and social celebrations. Throughout the country there are festivals every month, some of which last for days at a time.

In February the Carnival Festival is celebrated all across Bolivia. A parade with decorated cars and trucks, and hundreds of dancers, winds through the streets. In the largest celebration, in Oruro, the parade lasts for twelve hours. The dancers are dressed in ornate outfits, which take weeks to make. Adults and children of all ages take part in the dancing. For those not in the parade, there is an opportunity to throw water balloons and spray foam from cans in all directions. It often becomes a free-for-all, with children and young adults "shooting" anyone nearby.

In June people gather in La Paz to celebrate "El Gran Poder" with parades, dancing, music, and celebrating. The name of the festival comes from the neighborhood in La Paz through which the parade passes. Those participating in the parade walk, march, and dance the total distance of eight miles. The costumes and masks are very colorful and reflect Bolivia's history and legends.

dwarf household god of possessions and good luck, is believed to help those who please him. Each January, Bolivians buy tiny replicas of items they would like to have within the next year in hopes that Ekeko will help them obtain their desired possessions. Some miners believe that the areas underground belong to El Tio, the devil of the interior of the earth. At the entrance of many mines sits an image of El Tio. Miners leave gifts of coca leaves or cigarettes to please him so that they will be safe as they go down into his kingdom.

SPORTS

Nearly all Bolivians, like these altiplano women, love soccer. Every village has some sort of playing field, and Bolivians carefully follow the fortunes of their national team.

Although Bolivians work hard to provide for the needs of a family, they make time to enjoy various sports and leisure activities, strengthening the bonds between family and friends. Perhaps the second most unifying factor of Bolivian life—after religion—is the love of soccer. Nearly all groups of people and ages play soccer. Author Mark Cramer explains, " . . . from the indigenous highlands to the primeval jungles,

seemingly impenetrable cultural barriers break down when they play soccer with the locals."[27] Even small villages have dirt, sand, or cement playing fields. Much of the population follows the matches of the Bolivian national team. Bolivia enjoys the distinction of having the highest national stadium, where matches prove tougher for visiting teams not used to such high altitudes.

The Tahuichi Aguilera Academy of Bolivia in Santa Cruz enjoys international fame for its soccer training program for children from age six to age nineteen. To build endurance and leg strength, students run up sand dunes and run against the strong current of a river. The academy also keeps track of the educational progress and health of its students. One of the academy's most famous students, Marco Antonio Etcheverry, played for Bolivia, for Chile, and for Major League Soccer's the Washington United. He earned the nickname "El Diablo" (the Devil) reportedly because of his competitive spirit and evil temper.

Other sports played throughout Bolivia include basketball and volleyball. These sports have leagues with fierce competition. Local areas enjoy more specialized sports. In the Lake Titicaca region swimming races are held, which are a great challenge because of the icy cold water and high altitude. The traditional sport of *tinku*, a rather violent cross between bare-fisted boxing and professional wrestling, is seen mostly in remote villages near Potosí. Rodeos are considered an important sport in southern Bolivia near the Argentine border.

RECREATION AND LEISURE

Wealthier Bolivians living in and around La Paz enjoy golfing at the Malasilla Golf Club, the highest golf course in the world, where the ball travels farther than normal because of the thin air at that altitude. They also use the highest ski lift in the world at Chacaltaya, where skiers sometimes need to keep small oxygen tanks with them to help them breathe.

As most Bolivian families cannot afford expensive factory-made toys, children often make slingshots and wooden tops. In a game called *trumfo*, children try to hit a bottle cap with their spinning top. Young Bolivian boys enjoy playing marbles, while the girls are more interested in rhythmic clapping games.

Visiting the *peñas* is another favorite form of entertainment in the cities and villages. These informal music clubs

El Gran Poder is an extravagant folk festival celebrated in La Paz every June. Such festivals allow the Bolivian people to celebrate their distinct ethnicities.

play various styles of music, and customers sing along if they wish. Folk festivals play an important part in the life of all Bolivians. Many of the festivals began as religious celebrations, but have evolved into folk celebrations. These festivals combine ornate costumes, masks, dancing, and folk music. Adults and children often practice for weeks before dancing in these festivals. Daily life in Bolivia clearly shows that diverse groups of people can work hard, play hard, celebrate their ethnicity, and preserve the ways of the past.

THE ARTS IN BOLIVIA

The arts in Bolivia have been influenced by its various cultures and political movements. The diversity of Bolivia's people creates a full spectrum of artistic expression. As the Travelvantage website for Bolivia suggests, "The Aymara people's culture eventually fused with the Incas' and later, with that of the Spaniards. The result: a rich culture quite varied in the areas of sculpture, painting, literature, and architecture."[28] All three cultures display a reverence for spiritual and natural themes, which has filled all forms of Bolivian art throughout the centuries.

MUSIC OF THE ALTIPLANO

Music in a multitude of forms surrounds Bolivians throughout their lifetime. Young boys on the altiplano heights, given charge over the family's grazing animals, pass the time playing simple, handmade flutes. Families, friends, and communities kneel in worship together to the strains of violins and harps. And young people meet at local clubs to sing and dance to the latest popular songs. Bolivians also enjoy a great variety of music at religious festivals, town celebrations, and *peñas*. From traditional to classical to contemporary, the diversity in the style of music, as well as the instruments used and the setting in which it is played, gives full expression to the Indian, Hispanic, and blended cultures of Bolivia.

Haunting tunes played on wind instruments characterize the music of the altiplano. In the past only men played this music, and singing did not accompany it. Now lyrics are often added with themes of love, sorrow, and reflection. Women sometimes sing, but rarely play the instruments. The wind instruments are usually panpipes, made of reeds of different lengths, or *quenas*, a wooden flute, which is held like a clarinet. Groups as large as twenty people sometimes play panpipes together. Traditionally one tune was played by all the members of an ensemble, but now songs played in harmony

Musicians play traditional woodwind instruments, known as quenas, *at a festival in the city of Tarabuco.*

are common. "El Condor Pasa," a song recorded by Paul Simon, represents this style of traditional highland music.

Inti-Illimani, an internationally famous group, plays traditional highland music. This group of men, who met as engineering students at Santiago Technical University in the 1960s, weave elements of traditional Andean music together to produce all types of melodies. They began by searching for a sense of their own roots and for four decades have explored and revealed the indigenous cultures to their listeners. Inti-Illimani uses thirty different instruments to capture the essence of the Andes. Sting, Wynton Marsalis, and Bruce Springsteen have all played with Inti-Illimani, who have made over thirty recordings.

TRADITIONAL AND CLASSICAL MUSIC

A group called Savia Andina uses traditional music to protest social inequities. Their songs bring pressing social issues to light and lead the listener to consider his own place in the conflict, as a part of the problem or the solution. This five-man group uses panflutes, drums, *charangos*, and guitars to highlight the music of various Bolivian regions and cities.

Perhaps the most famous musicians within Bolivia are the *charango* players. In the hands of a talented player, these seemingly simple "little guitars" express the emotion of a song. Ernesto Cavour of La Paz and Mauro Nunez of Sucre each enjoy a huge following in Bolivia. The Museo de Arte Moderno in Sucre displays some of the *charangos* handmade by Nunez, while the Museo de Instrumentos Nativos in La Paz displays not only different types of *charangos*, but also many other native instruments.

In contrast to the haunting tunes of the altiplano, one hears the strong beat of drums and a powerful rhythm in the *yungas*, where descendants of African slaves live. The traditional music of the eastern and southern lowlands is greatly affected by the neighboring countries and the Spanish legacy. The salsa style of Brazil, the tango of Argentina, and the flamenco of Spain are all popular musical styles in the

The most famous musicians in Bolivia are charango *players (front). The* charango *resembles a miniature guitar.*

Santa Cruz and Chaco regions. All of these lowland styles use fast and lively rhythms.

Classical music concerts and operas take place in the largest cities. Bolivian Walter Ponce achieved a worldwide reputation as a piano soloist, earning praise for his concerts from Carnegie Hall to Morocco. His recitals for the BBC and Voice of America have been heard all over the world. He has also collaborated with another famous Bolivian musician, violinist and conductor Jaime Laredo. Laredo continues to receive international recognition, and his popularity in Bolivia has led to having a stadium named in his honor and his picture on a set of postage stamps.

A BLEND OF OLD AND NEW

Contemporary music in Bolivia includes brass bands and a blending of folk and jazz. Brass band music, which is characterized by strong melodies and regular rhythms, is often heard at festivals and celebrations throughout Bolivia. Most towns of any size develop at least a small band, which performs during parades, for local celebrations, and at weddings. They play many different types of music, from military marches to traditional love songs—whatever the occasion demands.

In addition a blending of folk music and jazz or rock has become popular at celebrations and at music and dance clubs. This blending of styles gained international fame with the group Los Kjarkas and uses a combination of many traditional and nontraditional instruments, such as keyboards

MUSICAL INSTRUMENTS

Bolivian music is played using many different kinds of instruments. In some areas cow horns, either used alone (*erke*) or attached to the end of a long pole (*cana*), are used as woodwind instruments. Trumpets made of shells can be heard at certain traditional celebrations. The *charango* guitar is made of an armadillo shell or wood, with ten strings. Wind instruments made of wood, sugarcane, bone, or ceramic sound like a flute. Guitars, violins, drums, and brass instruments round out the favorite instruments of Bolivians. At folk festivals and celebrations, many of these instruments are combined to highlight the full spectrum of Bolivian music.

and electric guitars. On weekends, bands play this music in many clubs in the larger cities.

Music and dancing go hand in hand in Bolivia. At every festival, dances are performed using steps passed down for generations, which combine aspects of the indigenous, Spanish, and African cultures. For many years, only men danced, but now nearly everyone joins in. The Diablada (Devil dance) performed at the time of Lent portrays victory over sin. To the music of drums, guitars, flutes, and *charangos*, people dance through the streets dressed in elaborate costumes and masks with horns, serpents, and jewels. Throughout the dance, the Devil and his wicked wife, China Supay, move in and out among men in costumes representing various sins. As the procession reaches the church, Saint Michael appears, destroying the sins with his sword and forcing them to remove their masks. This dance, and others that are performed at festivals throughout Bolivia, unite the people in a celebration of their traditions.

HISTORICAL LITERATURE

The literature of the Bolivian people, past and present, reflects their beliefs, struggles, and dreams. Beginning in precolonial times, when no written language existed, Bolivians passed on stories and histories through oral tradition. When the Spanish arrived, they tried to piece together the history and the traditional stories of both the Inca and the Aymara people. Over the centuries, Inca wise men, called *amantus*, had memorized and recounted their stories to each generation and eventually to the Spanish. However, it was more difficult to uncover the history of the Aymara people, as they retained only folktales and very little knowledge of their actual history. The *Nueva Historia de la Literature Boliviana* (1987) contains the most comprehensive collection of the oral histories of the Aymara and Inca. Author David Nelson Blair explains that traditional pre-Inca Aymara folktales "portray a world full of danger and deception. Souls are kidnapped; spells and counterspells are cast. Suspicion is deep, and trickster tales are common."[29]

During early colonial times, before the colony obtained printing presses, Bartolome Arzans de Orsua y Vela handwrote a chronicle of the town of Potosí. This chronicle covered the years from 1545 to 1736 and offers a very clear and

The Devil dance, known as the Diablada, is performed annually during Lent. The intricate dance symbolizes human victory over the temptation to sin.

complete view of daily colonial life. Parts of his historical account are published in a book called *The Tales of Potosí.* Other handwritten books from that period include Aymara and Inca grammar books and dictionaries compiled by Catholic priests. Written using the indigenous languages, these books give great insight into the precolonial cultures.

LITERATURE OF PROTEST

Beginning in 1880, a new type of writing began to emerge in which authors were not afraid to confront the inequities and concerns they saw in the Bolivian social and political systems. Before the 1880s Bolivian literature had been virtually all nonfiction. Now authors began to use both fiction and nonfiction to make their grievances known.

Nataniel Aguirre's classic novel of Bolivia's War of Independence, *Juan de la Rosa* (1889), compared the struggle of a young man from Cochabamba to Bolivia's fight for freedom. Aguirre used his novel to bring to light the cruel Spanish repression. Written from the perspective of an old man who took part in the War of Independence during his youth, and is now recounting those days of fierce resistance, it gives insight into the fears and hopes of the young and old who fought for freedom.

Ricardo Jaimes Freyre wrote about the exploitation of the Indians of Bolivia in *Indian Justice* (1907). This work showed the arrogance and evil of the wealthy landowners, and the simple goodness of the indigenous people. Freyre also wrote historical books, dramas, and poetry. As the first Bolivian poet to gain international recognition, he used this fame to heighten the awareness of the world to the social concerns in South America.

One of Bolivia's most famous novelists, Augusto Cespedes, wrote The Devil's Metal *in 1946 to expose the terrible working conditions in the country's tin mines.*

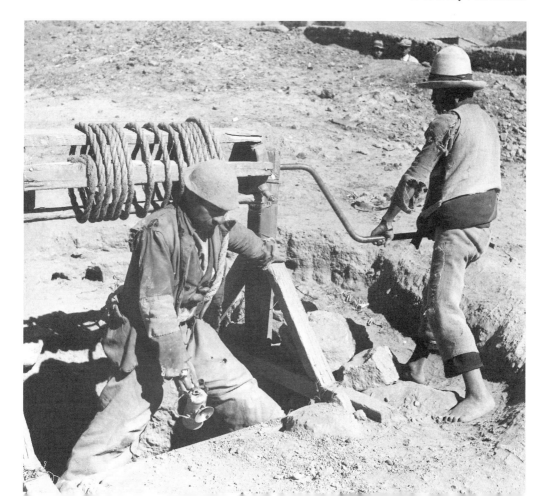

Following the 1932–1935 Chaco War, many writers began to shed even greater light on the problems of Bolivia. James M. Malloy contends, "By protest they hoped to publicize the faults of their homeland and to use literature as a propagandistic weapon."[30] In *Mestizo Blood* (1936), Augusto Cespedes criticized the Bolivian government, which he felt brought on the Chaco War. Written to expose the terrible conditions of miners and to encourage nationalization of the tin mines, his book *The Devil's Metal* (1946) became one of Bolivia's best-known novels. As a lawyer and a journalist, Cespedes used his position to persuade Bolivians of the need for social and political change.

Scathing descriptions of the owners of rubber plantations and their exploitation of the rubber workers are seen in *Borrachera Verde* (1938), by Raul Botelho Gosalvez. In *Altiplano* (1945) he wrote of the desperate situation of many highland families, who were only one poor harvest away from starvation. These books, and others which clearly exhibited the need for governmental, social, and economic change in Bolivia, set the stage for the Revolution of 1952. More and more Bolivians began to see their country's problems through the eyes of these writers.

CONTEMPORARY LITERATURE

Contemporary Bolivian literature continues to address social issues, as well as a wide spectrum of other themes. Yolanda Bedregal, nicknamed "Yolanda of Bolivia," gained international recognition as a poet, short story writer, and novelist. She attained fame for works like *Under the Dark Sun* (1971) in which a young woman is killed in a Bolivian uprising. Her poems and stories often include mysticism, involving the influence of the spirit world. Bedregal's writings also include nonfiction works on art and history, as well as books for children.

Jaime Saenz is considered by some as Bolivia's greatest writer of the twentieth century, in part because he presented contemporary problems in a realistic way. Saenz created works in both poetry and prose, writing fiction and nonfiction. His best-known poetry is written in free verse. *As the Comet Passes* (1982), a collection of poems, explores themes of love, death, the human spirit, and modern social issues.

ARCHITECTURE

The majority of great Bolivian architecture is ancient rather than modern. The pre-Inca ruins at Tiwanaku exhibit advanced stonework and carving, and indicate that Indians had the ability to move and set up blocks of stone weighing many tons. In addition structures with polygonal stones fit together perfectly without mortar, and intricate carvings amaze those who view later Inca ruins. Excavation at these and other sites in the eastern regions of Bolivia continue to uncover highly developed architectural skill in these pre-colonial cultures.

During the colonial period, the vast wealth from the silver mines paid for the building of many beautiful churches. The various building styles included Renaissance, baroque, and the Mestizo style, which used a mixture of images from Christianity and the indigenous religions. "From a distance, Bolivian colonial buildings are Spanish, from an arm's length they are distinctly Indian,"[31] explains Blair. Renaissance churches included courtyards and simple designs, while baroque churches formed the shape of a cross and had domes. From churches of the simplest adobe style to ornately carved stone, from the large Churrignerique Church in Potosí to smaller Bavarian-style wooden churches in the lowlands, these places of worship reflected both the period of their construction and the materials at hand.

As the Spanish built churches, they also established towns in the Spanish style. For example, the villages generally enclosed a central plaza. Although some of these colonial buildings are now decaying reminders of wealthier days of the past, some are preserved with the same beauty as when they were built. The central area of the city of Sucre showcases some of this colonial architecture, with its white-washed, two-story buildings and narrow balconies.

Early examples of Bolivia's modern architecture include the Palace of Justice in La Paz and the Palace of Government in Sucre, which were built at the end of the nineteenth century and are very ornate with pillars, marble, and balconies. During the 1930s, Bolivian architecture moved to a more functional style of buildings characterized by simple designs. At this time, architect Emilio Villanueva based his work on the ancient architecture of the Tiwanakan culture, with simple stonework. During the 1970s, Gustavo Medeiros designed

The Presidential Palace in La Paz exhibits the elaborate ornamentation used on buildings that were constructed in Bolivia during the late 1800s.

modernist buildings using exposed concrete and brick. He designed his architecture around the landscape, building against canyon walls or other natural features. Juan Carlos Calderon, one of Bolivia's best-known architects, is currently in great demand as the economy can now support new development and construction.

ANCIENT ART AND WEAVINGS

From the precious metals fashioned by skilled craftsmen millennia ago to contemporary works in paint, in stone, and on film, Bolivians have created a wealth of beauty in the visual arts. The use of ceramics, silver, gold, stone, and wood characterize the art of precolonial times. These included religious, decorative, and functional items such as jars and cups. Many of these Aymara and Inca treasures were lost to the Spanish during the colonial days. The pieces in gold and silver that were not considered works of art were, in many cases, melted down by the Spanish. Fortunately, some works survived, and a good collection of ceramics, copper, silver, and gold can be seen at the Museo de Metales Preciosos Pre-Columbinos in La Paz. Artifacts from as early as 15,000 B.C. are displayed at the Museo Arqueologico in Cochabamba.

Woven fabrics were so highly prized during the Inca period that they were used in offerings to the Inca gods. The few surviving examples of beautifully woven fabrics from that period display very intricate designs and skilled craftsmanship. Today in Bolivia textiles are prized for both their practical and artistic value. The patterns and colors used by weavers are distinct to each region. The artisans around Sucre produce some of the world's finest weavings, and the city's Museo Textil Etnografico displays these woven works of art.

THE ART OF SPINNING AND WEAVING

A common thread running through the culture of Bolivia remains the ancient art of spinning wool and weaving fabric. The process begins with the gathering of the wool from the sheep, llamas, or alpacas. After cleaning the wool, the fibers are separated and the wool is spun into a single, thick thread. Two strands are then combined; the yarn is dyed and spun one last time. Fibers spun in this way have great strength and are very smooth.

The actual weaving can take weeks to complete, and the fabric can then be used in clothing, headbands, pouches, as blankets, or as the rectangular cloth that women use to carry items on their back. The town of Potolo excels in the production of red and black textiles with animal designs, while throughout Bolivia the use of blue wool signifies mourning. The variety of amazing textiles produced within Bolivia gives a very literal picture of the phrase "beauty in diversity."

Spinning wool (pictured) and weaving fabric are ancient Bolivian traditions.

PAINTINGS AND SCULPTURES

Colonial works of art include oil paintings of religious subjects and a few portraits of famous people, generally commissioned by wealthy silver mine owners. In the early eighteenth century, Melchor Perez Holguin, known as the "Golden Paintbrush," painted saints, priests, and monks with very sharp facial features and beautifully detailed clothing. The Royal Mint in Potosí displays many of his works.

Cecilio Guzman de Rojas (1900–1951), often called the father of contemporary Bolivian art, studied in Spain for ten years and then returned to Bolivia. In his painting, he sought to depict indigenous people in natural settings. As a teacher in La Paz, he greatly influenced the next generation of Bolivian artists, as they imitated his style and themes. Beginning in the 1950s, abstract painting became more popular with artists like Maria Luisa Pacheco and Oscar Pantoja. Although their style was different from Guzman de Rojas's, they continued the use of indigenous subjects.

Colonial Bolivian paintings, like this seventeenth-century work, are typically portraits of wealthy silver mine owners.

In the realm of sculpture, Marina Núñez del Prado (1912–1996), perhaps Bolivia's best-known modern artist, created sculptures in wood, granite, alabaster, basalt, and white onyx. She often used indigenous Bolivian motifs with Indian women and children. In addition to the beauty of her sculptures, she is famous for the sheer volume of her work, having produced hundreds of sculptures over the course of her lifetime. Her abstract works are representative of modern Bolivian art.

CINEMA

Unlike the other arts, the development of cinematic expression in Bolivia has been relatively recent. Bolivian movies are known for making political and social statements. Oscar Sori and Antonio Equino produced a movie called *From El Alto to Calacoto* in which Aymara dialogue highlights the economic, social, and cultural diversity among contemporary Bolivians. El Alto, the city of cold nights and poverty, is used in contrast to the beautiful, exclusive mansions and wealth of La Paz. James Carlos Valdivia's documentaries and his television series *La Vida en al Espejo* (Life in the Mirror) have made his name well-known within the country and in Mexico, where his television series is shown.

Perhaps the best-known Bolivian filmmaker is La Paz native Jac Avila. After furthering his studies in film and photography in New York at St. John's University and Germain School of Photography, he honed his skills of producing, directing, and editing. His film about Haiti, *"Krik? Krik! Tales of a Nightmare,"* conveys Avila's message of the struggles of life in Haiti with powerful images and simplicity. His film production company, Pachamama Films, produces feature films, miniseries, and documentaries in Bolivia. Avila produced and directed *El Hombre de la Luna* (The Man in the Moon), a five-part murder mystery, and the feature film *Paloma.* In addition to his work for Telenovela Pachamama, a division of Pachamama Films, he serves as an instructor at Catholic University in Bolivia, influencing the Bolivian filmmakers of the future.

The arts of Bolivia mirror the history of the region—from the past, with its works reflecting distinct ethnic groups, to the present, in a mingling of the various styles. While the ancient themes are still honored in contemporary Bolivian art, the nation is also using music, literature, and cinema to examine issues facing Bolivians now and in the future.

6

COMPLEX CHALLENGES

Bolivia faces a daunting task as it deals with great challenges. Many of these issues are interrelated, tied to poverty and the frustration that poverty brings. According to author Mark Cramer, "Bolivia is a country with grave problems, most of them economic, inherited from her colonial past."[32] Bolivia is searching for ways to build a strong, sustainable economic foundation. This will encourage responsible foreign investments, bringing in money to address the pressing needs of its people.

NATIONAL ECONOMY

Bolivia considers those who live on an income of less than sixty dollars a month to be below the poverty level, and 65 percent of its people are in that category, making it the poorest nation in South America. Bolivia struggles with a cycle of high inflation as well. Foreign investments and aid could address both of these situations, but because of the unstable economy, foreign investors hesitate to set up businesses or provide money. Bolivia's past political instability, although recently more calm, also frightens investors away. Investors need assurances that the government currently in power, which cooperates with them, will not be overthrown by one that will not.

Steps to increase the amount of foreign investment include the 1994 Law of Capitalization, which began a process of allowing foreign investors to own up to 50 percent of Bolivian companies which had previously been state-owned. This move toward a more open free-market system has brought billions of dollars into Bolivia. Without these investments, increased exportation, expansion of industry, and general economic growth remain nearly impossible for a country as poor as Bolivia. Critics of the program urge the government to ensure that Bolivians, not just the foreign companies, benefit from this arrangement.

Money has been poured into the mining industry, at the expense of other industries and businesses, for generations. In order to expand and stabilize its economy, Bolivia has begun to decrease its dependence on mining. Because the price of mined metal continually rises and falls on the international market, Bolivia has begun to increase the production of other products for which prices do not vary as much. While zinc mining currently holds an important place in Bolivia's economy, new technology-based computer and telecommunications businesses could be developed to both increase Bolivia's exports and to aid the nation in becoming more technologically advanced.

The strength of Bolivia's economy also depends on both increasing the production of goods and insuring the ability to move these products to markets. The use of new methods and machinery in agriculture and manufacturing could increase the nation's goods for export. Bolivia's oil and gas reserves may provide the greatest boost to its economy in the coming years, if the nation focuses its attention and resources on refining and other related industries, including plastics and paint.

To help expand and stabilize Bolivia's economy, the government has reduced its reliance on the revenues from the mining industry in recent years.

MAKING A DIFFERENCE

Nongovernmental organizations (NGOs) and nonprofit agencies within poorer countries meet social, physical, and economic needs. These organizations can be charities, foundations, or religious groups. Projects often include promoting or improving reading, alleviating hunger, improving agricultural methods, and meeting health needs—anything which lessens the poverty of the people or the problems that come as a result of that poverty.

NGOs are often more flexible than government agencies and can therefore address specific needs which might not be met otherwise. While governmental agencies deal with national concerns and have an extensive bureaucracy, NGOs can move more quickly to meet needs.

In Bolivia, NGOs and nonprofit agencies are involved in everything from promoting the marketing of llama meat near Lake Titicaca to providing safe drinking water in Santa Cruz and the altiplano. The nonprofit Eco-Bolivia Foundation helps finance the Madidi National Park, while the Quesimpuco Health Foundation, a Christian nonprofit organization, provides health care for the poor in the Andes village of Quesimpuco. These agencies are making a positive difference in the lives of Bolivians.

To move these products quickly and efficiently to national and international markets, improvement of all modes of transportation demands a high priority. Bolivia's road system needs expansion, the railroad system needs updating and regular maintenance, and the runways of small airports must be lengthened to handle larger planes.

International trade agreements are necessary to improve the Bolivian economy. As a member of MERCOSUR (El Mercado Comun del Sur), Bolivia benefits from trade agreements with its South American neighbors. International leaders are discussing ways to improve trade and to strengthen the economies of poorer countries like Bolivia. They have agreed that by 2006, NAFTA (North American Free Trade Agreement), which develops trade agreements between Canada, Mexico, and the United States, will expand to include South American nations.

Much needed financial aid has boosted Bolivia's economy as well. In 1991, the United States forgave Bolivia's debts totaling nearly $366 million. In 1998 the Heavily Indebted Poor Country (HIPC) program gave loans of $450 million to Bolivia, with the provision that they need not be repaid if certain economic and social improvements are made. Some Bolivians worry that accepting such aid carries with it too many restrictions and demands. However, with Bolivia's desperate economic situation, this aid can hardly be refused.

PERSONAL POVERTY

The struggles of Bolivia's economy are lived out each day on a very personal level by the majority of Bolivian people. Rural areas exhibit the worst poverty, where life remains generally unchanged from one hundred years ago. These rural poor, almost exclusively of Indian descent, live on small plots of land, harvesting just enough to meet their needs. The Popular Participation Program, initiated by the Bolivian government in 1994, strives to direct money to the most impoverished rural communities, sorely neglected in the past. Surprisingly, this government program, designed to be a windfall for the nation's most impoverished, met with distrust from the Indians. Having never received such economic help, they feared that the government would require something in return. This program has made positive steps as poor communities have directed the finances toward projects most important to them. Still, the crushing rural poverty forces many to move to the cities, where an explosion of shantytowns with plywood shacks and inadequate sewers develops.

This great poverty, and the frustration and the desperation it brings, often results in an increase in crime—much of which can be related to illegal drug trafficking and corruption at all levels. The illegal export of coca for use in manufacturing cocaine yields billions of dollars each year and provides an estimated 350,000 jobs. To counteract this, Bolivia receives billions in aid from the United States to eradicate coca crops. However, putting an end to the crime and corruption that occurs, from the growers all the way up to the bribed government officials, seems an almost impossible task. Bolivia continues to address this by finding and prosecuting those who are involved in the trafficking, as well as officials who fill their pockets with money for ignoring this activity.

A shantytown overlooks the city of La Paz. Many Bolivians in both urban settings and rural communities live in poverty.

INTERNAL UNREST

The internal unrest in Bolivia generally finds its source in political differences and poverty. Even the political rivalries basically stem from differences in beliefs about how Bolivia's limited economic resources should be spent. While the damaging violent political upheavals of the past have decreased, the unrest of various groups continues to boil below the surface, and sometimes explodes.

At the beginning of the twenty-first century, Bolivia sought foreign investors to bolster its economy. One company leased the water rights to serve over five hundred thousand people in the Cochabamba area and immediately doubled the residents' water rate. Protests against this increased charge began as peaceful marches, but turned violent as protest leaders were arrested and riot police used tear gas.

On April 8, 2000, President Hugo Banzer Suarez declared a state of emergency forbidding gatherings of more than four people, taking over the radio stations, and bringing in soldiers to occupy the city's center. After a week of violence, an agreement was signed releasing those who had been arrested, forcing the company out of Bolivia, and giving financial compensation to the families of the six people who had been killed.

Another riot occurred in January 2002, when thousands of coca growers gathered in Cochabamba to protest the government's arrest of their leaders and destruction of their crops. The protesters called for a nationwide road blockade to cripple the nation and to force the government to release those who had been arrested. In the days that followed, the demonstrations in Cochabamba's central plaza grew in size and fury. Police fired tear gas and rubber pellets at the people. Protesters set up burning barricades in the streets, and violence escalated on both sides. By the time an agreement

Bolivian soldiers walk past an area where coca dries in the sun. Coca growers began rioting in 2002 when the government destroyed their crops.

was reached three weeks after the protests began, ten people had died and more than one hundred had been injured.

Protests over poor wages and working conditions often leads to strikes in many occupations, from mining to teaching, which sometimes result in violence. In February 2003, protests in La Paz turned violent after three weeks of strikes and roadblocks. The protesters demanded raises for teachers, the end of the destruction of coca, and the withdrawal of a proposed water tax. In the ensuing violence, sixteen people died and dozens were injured. Protesters burned government offices, and Bolivia's cabinet resigned. To ensure his safety, President Gonzalo Sánchez de Lozada secretly left the Presidential Palace in an ambulance. Compromises between the government and the protesters finally ended the violence.

Unfortunately, the protests and violence that forced President Sánchez de Lozada from office in October 2003 continued the pattern of civil and political unrest. The protests

Coca growers blockade a highway in January 2003 to protest the government's continued destruction of their crops.

ended after President Sánchez de Lozada resigned and Vice President Carlos Mesa promised to call for a referendum, or a vote, in which the Bolivians could decide whether they wanted to approve the natural gas sale to the United States.

Health

Disease and health challenges plague the Bolivian people and contribute to a lower life expectancy as compared to other nations. Bolivian men live an average of sixty-two years, with women living sixty-seven years. This is about twelve years less than those living in the United States. Only 40 percent of the population has access to health care. Few doctors, nurses, or health facilities serve the rural areas or the outskirts of Bolivia's cities. This lack of available health care and the poverty of many people contribute to Bolivia's greatest health problems: poor nutrition, tuberculosis and other lung diseases, and a high infant mortality rate.

Lack of prenatal care directly affects Bolivia's infant mortality rate—the highest in South America. Bolivia also has the highest percentage of low birth-weight babies. Eighty-three out of every one thousand babies do not live to their first birthday. Since the majority of areas lack prenatal care, some conditions that could be discovered before birth go undetected. Additionally, in poorer Bolivian families, babies are often born at home with little consideration for sterile conditions. If a problem arises during the birth, the baby often dies.

An estimated 30 to 40 percent of Bolivians suffer from malnutrition. The diet of the poorest citizens includes only what grows in their region or what they can grow themselves. Lack of calcium, vitamins, protein, and the necessary number of calories all contribute to serious medical problems. Many develop protein deficiencies, resulting in muscle weakness (including the heart), impaired brain development, and learning difficulties. The lack of iodine in the diet results in goiter, the enlargement of the thyroid gland, causing swelling in the neck. During a woman's pregnancy, this condition can cause retardation in the baby. Bolivia holds the highest rate of stunted growth for small children, presumably because of this poor nutrition. When milk is not readily available, mothers feed their small children crushed corn with water. Unfortunately, undernourished children and adults are more vulnerable to infection and diseases, including tuberculosis.

As a result of malnutrition, poverty, and the lack of health care, preventable or treatable diseases take their toll on the population. Tuberculosis is a deadly lung disease that spreads through contact with infected people. Although treatments and vaccinations are available, it often goes undiagnosed and untreated. Other lung diseases, such as silica, result from breathing the dust produced in mining operations. In silica, breathing becomes more and more difficult, eventually causing death. Simple precautions such as using protective face masks could decrease the amount of dust taken into the lungs, but many cannot afford them.

Dysentery, a bacterial infection that causes severe diarrhea and dehydration, often results from drinking unclean water or eating contaminated food. This problem plagues residents in both rural areas and in cities that do not have access to clean water. Raw sewage often runs into streams and rivers, whose water may be used for cooking and drinking. One of the major causes of the high death rate for babies is dysentery. Bolivia's government is seeking to make water available to more citizens as well as improve the quality of the water supply. International agencies and nongovernmental organizations (NGOs) also have made this a priority and are helping Bolivia meet this important challenge.

Chagas' disease, which afflicts 25 percent of Bolivians, results from the bite of the *vinchuca* beetle. This type of beetle often makes its home in the thatch of a roof or the cracks in the mud walls of homes. The disease causes increasing strain on the heart over a number of years, eventually causing death. To slow the incidence of the disease, houses can be treated with insecticides and thatch can be replaced with metal roofs. Since it is also transmitted through blood transfusions, systems are being set up for better screening of the nation's blood supply. A task force has been established to study Chagas' disease, attempting to eliminate the threat by 2010.

EDUCATION

Although major steps have been taken to improve the educational system in Bolivia, much need for reform remains. In

this poor nation, the estimated 5 percent of the budget set aside for education does not sufficiently meet the educational needs of its people. Bolivia holds one of the lowest literacy rates in South America, with 13 percent of its people unable to read. This may be because most schools teach only in Spanish, putting the Indian children who speak other languages at a distinct disadvantage. In addition few supplies and poor pay frustrate teachers and cause many strikes, leaving schools empty for days and weeks.

These children live in the squalor of a mining community near Potosí.

The need for children and young people to help tend their family farms or earn money has a negative effect on school attendance, especially in rural areas. Only 33 percent of those beginning first grade will finish fifth grade. The dropout rate is highest among girls, who are more likely to stay home to care for younger siblings, and rural children, with only 40 percent of rural children going past the third grade. Twenty percent of young Bolivians start high school, with about 5 percent beginning college and 1 percent graduating.

Recent reforms address some of these concerns. In some areas classes are being taught in both Spanish and the indigenous language. Adult reading classes are doing their part to improve literacy. Additional economic aid now goes to the poorest communities to buy supplies and books as well as to add libraries to the schools. As these positive steps show results, the government is more likely to invest more time and money to improve the education of all Bolivians.

Bolivia has one of the lowest literacy rates in South America. For those children who do attend school, little money is available for books and supplies.

DEVELOPMENT

Bolivia struggles to find a responsible balance between economic progress and the protection of its natural resources. Exploiting these resources seems to answer the economic problems facing the country. However, unbridled development destroys the beauty and ecological wealth that make Bolivia so unique. Author Deanna Swaney notes that with "potential fortunes to be made in minerals, agricultural opportunities and forest products, conservation isn't as convenient as it once was. With so many economic advantages, there's unfortunately little incentive to consider long-term effects."[33]

This conflict becomes most evident in the rain forest region. The slash-and-burn method of clearing the land continues in spite of evidence that it destroys the land's productivity for years at a time. Clearing vast tracts of the rain forest, by any method, causes serious erosion, with soil and its nutrients flooding into the rivers and the streams. To many Bolivians concerned with the financial needs of their nation, the development of ranches, industries, mines, and electricity sounds wise. But to those concerned about the damage, it is a frightening prospect. The concerns are not only for the loss of vegetation native to the rain forest, but also the loss of the rain forest habitat for the wildlife and the indigenous population. With the reduction of plant and animal life, the people who live off that land must move on, losing their unique way of life.

CONSERVATION

To conserve its resources, Bolivia has begun to embrace ecotourism, which works to bring tourists to the rain forest without damaging the natural habitat. The companies that promote ecotourism seek to improve the local economy by bringing in profits while protecting the environment. By limiting the number of tourists and by requiring that they leave the environment exactly the way they found it, damage to the rain forest is minimized.

Contamination of the land and the water by mining and other industries also concerns environmentalists. The

RAIN FOREST CONSERVATION

Bolivians and ecologists around the world are searching for ways to protect the Bolivian rain forest. To strengthen Bolivia's economy, money has poured in from the United States and Japan, from the World Bank and the International Monetary Fund (IMF), and from private corporations and military interests. Much of it is going toward the development of a road system to open the rain forest area and encourage economic growth through development. Critics suggest, however, that these funds are bringing in too much development and will destroy the rain forest.

Ecologists recommend that thousands of acres of land be set aside and be left untouched as reserves for the exclusive use of the indigenous people. They feel that the harvesting of timber and the construction of roads must be tightly controlled and severely limited. They suggest that some of the money coming into the country should be used to pay the Bolivian government to protect millions of rain forest acres.

These debates will, no doubt, continue far into the future, as the difficult question remains how best to protect the rain forest and still produce revenues for the people of that region and for the nation of Bolivia.

residue left by the mining process has destroyed some water sources and has damaged the soil. Companies are now required to clean up some of this and limit any damage done in the future. However, mining companies complain that the regulated cleanup costs and restrictions make it so expensive for them to extract the ore that they are not able to produce as much as they have in the past.

To protect Bolivia's valuable natural resources, many acres have been set aside over the past twenty years through the establishment of national parks and protected areas. This land is reserved for indigenous groups to protect them and their way of life. In an interesting approach aimed at helping Bolivia protect its natural resources, U.S.–based Conservation International paid off $650,000 of Bolivia's foreign debt in exchange for Bolivia's promise to permanently pro-

Bolivians shop at an open-air market in the altiplano. Today, Bolivia is faced with the task of creating sufficient arable land while preserving precious natural resources.

tect the 825,474-acre Reserva Biosferica del Beni. Located
northeast of La Paz, this nature reserve was created, in part,
to protect the land from development.

With potential for improvements in the struggling Bolivian economy, the nation must move ahead cautiously. No
simple answers will meet both the current and future concerns of this country. The recent unrest has further compli-
cated the challenges of strengthening Bolivia's economy and
meeting the needs of its citizens. The people of Bolivia see
the importance of coming together to deal with economic
and social issues, while still respecting their cultural differences. As they balance their traditions of the past with the
necessities of the present, they can work together to unify the
many people of Bolivia.

Facts About Bolivia

Government

Name: Republic of Bolivia

Government type: republic

Capitals: La Paz—seat of government; Sucre—seat of judiciary

Administrative divisions: nine departments

Independence: August 6, 1825

Executive Branch:
President: elected by popular vote to a five-year term
Cabinet: appointed by the president

Legislative Branch: National Congress has two houses—Chamber of Deputies (130 members) and Chamber of Senators (twenty-seven members, three from each department)

Judicial Branch: Supreme Court—twelve judges selected by National Congress

Geography

Area: 424,165 sq. miles (1,098,581 sq. km.)

Bordering countries: Brazil, Peru, Chile, Argentina, Paraguay

Climate: varies from frigid to tropical to desert

Terrain: high mountains, high plateau, foothills, jungle, low plains

Elevation extremes: 300 ft. (91 m.) to 21,463 ft. (6,542 m.)

Natural resources: antimony, tin, tungsten, gold, silver, zinc, iron, gas, oil, timber

Environmental issues: water pollution, deforestation, overgrazing

People

Population: 8,445,134

Population growth: 1.69 percent

Birth rate: 26.4/1000 population

Death rate: 8.1/1,000 population

Infant mortality rate: 58 deaths/1,000 live births

Life expectancy at birth: 64.8 years

Ethnic Groups:
Mestizo: 35 percent
Quechua: 30 percent
Aymara: 25 percent

White: 7 percent
Other: 3 percent

Religion:
Roman Catholic: 95 percent
Other: 5 percent

Official languages: Spanish, Quechua, Aymara

Literacy:
Total population: 87 percent
Male: 90 percent
Female: 84 percent

ECONOMY

Gross domestic product (GDP): $8.3 billion

GDP growth rate: 4.75 percent

GDP per capita: $990

GDP by sector:
Agriculture, forestry, fishing: 22 percent
Industry: 15.3 percent
Services: 62.7 percent

Population below poverty level: 65 percent

Inflation rate: 4.39 percent

Unemployment rate: 8 percent

Budget:
Revenues: $1,384 million
Expenditures: $1,921 million

Industries: mining, petroleum, textiles, clothing, food processing

Agricultural products: coffee, cotton, sugarcane, rice, wheat, potatoes,
coca, fish, beef, dairy products, wool

Exports: 1,282.97 million

Imports: 2,386.79 million

Currency: Boliviano (7.7 = 1 U.S. dollar)

NOTES

INTRODUCTION: A NATION OF DIVERSITY

1. Quoted in Thomas Rourke, *Man of Glory: Simón Bolívar.* New York: William Morrow, 1939, p. 205.

CHAPTER 1: A DIVERSE TOPOGRAPHY

2. Mark Cramer, *Culture Shock! Bolivia.* Portland: Graphic Arts Center Publishing, 2001, p. 10.

3. Quoted in Deanna Swaney, *Bolivia: A Lonely Planet Travel Survival Kit.* Oakland, CA: Lonely Planet Publications, 1996, p. 264.

4. Swaney, *Bolivia*, p. 228.

5. Cramer, *Culture Shock! Bolivia*, p. 15.

6. Rex A. Hudson, ed., *Bolivia: A Country Study.* Washington, DC: Library of Congress, Federal Research Division, 1991, p. 55.

7. Cramer, *Culture Shock! Bolivia*, p. 17.

CHAPTER 2: INVASIONS AND INDEPENDENCE

8. Maria Rostworowski de Diez Canseco, *History of the Inca Realm.* New York: Cambridge University Press, 1999, p. 67.

9. Herbert S. Klein, *Bolivia: The Evolution of a Multi-Ethnic Society.* New York: Oxford University Press, 1992, p. 17.

10. Quoted in Rostworowski, *History of the Inca Realm*, p. 41.

11. Magnus Morner, *The Andean Past: Land, Societies, and Conflicts.* New York: Columbia University Press, 1985, p. 22.

12. Rostworowski, *History of the Inca Realm*, p. 225.

13. Rostworowski, *History of the Inca Realm*, p. 67.

14. Klein, *Bolivia*, p. 76.

15. Klein, *Bolivia*, p. 92.

Chapter 3: The Challenges of Independence

16. Hudson, *Bolivia*, p. 17.

17. Quoted in Rourke, *Man of Glory*, p. 345.

18. Swaney, *Bolivia*, p. 14.

19. Julian Duguid, *Green Hell.* New York: Century, 1931, p. 58.

20. Klein, *Bolivia*, p. 185.

21. Klein, *Bolivia*, p. 187.

22. Morner, *The Andean Past*, p. 205.

Chapter 4: Daily Life in Bolivia

23. Hudson, *Bolivia*, p. 58.

24. Hudson, *Bolivia* p. xviii.

25. Quoted in Tatiana Pina, "Art Student Strives to Preserve the Traditions of His People," *Providence Journal*, May 10, 2001, p. 8.

26. Hudson, *Bolivia*, p. 52.

27. Cramer, *Culture Shock! Bolivia*, p. 178.

Chapter 5: The Arts in Bolivia

28. Travelvantage, "Bolivia." www.travelvantage.com.

29. David Nelson Blair, *The Land and People of Bolivia.* New York: J.B. Lippincott, 1990, p. 124.

30. James M. Malloy and Richard S. Thorn, eds., *Beyond the Revolution: Bolivia Since 1952.* Pittsburgh: University of Pittsburgh Press, 1971, p. 344.

31. Blair, *The Land and People of Bolivia*, p. 118.

Chapter 6: Complex Challenges

32. Cramer, *Culture Shock! Bolivia*, p. 11.

33. Swaney, *Bolivia*, p. 22.

GLOSSARY

alpaca: Domesticated animal of camel family; its wool used in clothing.

altiplano: High plateau.

amantu: Wise men who memorized and passed on stories and history of the Inca.

ayllu: Self-governing, clanlike group who exchanged labor and goods.

Aymara: Pre-Inca highland people.

Chaco: Hot, southeastern area of Bolivia.

cha'lla: Ritual offering or blessing to ask favor of the gods.

charango: Small guitarlike instrument used in traditional highland music.

Cholas: Term for Indian who has taken on Spanish mannerisms and dress.

conquistadores: Spaniards who defeated the Inca.

cordillera: Mountain range.

Criolla: Spanish citizen born in South America.

indigenous: Original inhabitants of an area.

Mestizo: Person having both Indian and Spanish blood.

mita: System that required communities to give labor to serve the state.

mitmaq: Persons sent by the state to a distant location to serve the state.

montaña: Foothills to the east and south of the Andes.

Oriente: Eastern regions of Bolivia.

Pachamama: Earth Mother.

padrino: Godparent.

peña: Informal folk-music club.

plaza: Square at the center of town.

Quechua: Language or descendants of the Inca.

quinoa: Highly nutritious grain.

reciprocity: System of giving gifts to insure loyalty.

soroche: Altitude sickness.

totora: A reed found near Lake Titicaca that is used as building material.

yungas: Foothills to the east and north of the Andes.

CHRONOLOGY

600 B.C.
Tiwanakan culture develops and flourishes.

A.D. 1200
Tiwanakan nation disappears near Lake Titicaca.

1200–1438
Rise of Aymara kingdom.

1460s
Inca conquest of Aymara kingdom.

1470
Aymara revolt against the Inca.

1532
Spanish arrive in Peru.

1533
Inca leader Atahuallpa killed by Spanish.

1544
Indian peasant discovers silver near present-day Potosí.

1548
La Paz is founded.

1780–1782
Tupac Amaru rebellion.

1809
Rebellion for independence in La Paz.

1809–1825
Wars of Independence in Upper Peru (Bolivia).

1825
Bolivia is declared a republic on August 6.

1826
Bolivia's first constitution is approved.

1829–1839
Government of Andrés de Santa Cruz.

1850s
Beginning of modern silver mining industry.

1879–1883
War of the Pacific; Bolivia loses Pacific Coast to Chile.

1880–1910
Rubber boom in Amazon basin.

1902
Tin replaces silver as major export.

1932–1935
Chaco War against Paraguay; Bolivia loses twenty thousand square miles in the Chaco region.

1952
Revolution of 1952; Victor Paz Estenssoro—leader of Nationalist Revolutionary Movement—becomes president and institutes reforms.

1985–1989
President Estenssoro brings dramatic reform.

1990
Four million acres of rain forest land allocated to indigenous peoples.

1994
President Gonzalo Sánchez de Lozada expands privatization and institutes the Popular Participation Program.

1997
Plan instituted to eradicate coca cultivation; Bolivia is included in HIPC debt-relief program; forms trade agreements with other South American countries.

2002
Gonzalo Sánchez de Lozada becomes president for second time.

2003
Violent protests in La Paz, with deaths and injuries; President Gonzalo Sánchez de Lozada resigns; Vice President Carlos Mesa assumes presidency.

FOR FURTHER READING

BOOKS

Bartolome Arzans de Orsua y Vela, *Tales of Potosí*. Providence, RI: Brown University Press, 1975. Stories and historical data from colonial Potosí.

Vicki Cobb, *This Place Is High: The Andes Mountains of South America*. New York: Walker, 1993. Describes what it is like to make a home in the Andes.

Yossi Ghinsberg, *The Harrowing Life-and-Death Story of Survival in the Amazon Rainforest*. New York: Random House, 1993. A story of being lost and alone in the depths of the rain forest.

Waltraud Q. Morales, *A Brief History of Bolivia*. New York: Facts On File, 2003. Provides background material on all aspects of Bolivia.

Allyn Stearman, *San Rafael, Camba Town: Life in a Lowland Bolivian Peasant Community*. Prospect Heights, IL: Waveland Press, 1995. Describes life in a remote village of eastern Bolivia.

PERIODICALS

Bryan Hodgson, "Simón Bolívar," *National Geographic*, March 1994.

Johan Reinhard, "Sacred Peaks of the Andes," *National Geographic*, March 1992.

WEBSITES

Bolivia Web Interactive (www.boliviaweb.com). Provides extensive information on the nation and people of Bolivia.

Aymara Uta (www.aymara.org). A good source of information specific to Aymaran Bolivians.

CIA: The World Factbook (www.cia.gov). In-depth information on Bolivia.

103

WORKS CONSULTED

BOOKS

David Nelson Blair. *The Land and People of Bolivia.* New York: J.B. Lippincott, 1990. Shares insights into the past, present, and future of Bolivia's land and cultures.

Mark Cramer, *Culture Shock! Bolivia.* Portland: Graphic Arts Center Publishing, 2001. Examines current Bolivian customs, culture, and conflicts. Offers practical advice for visitors.

Julian Duguid, *Green Hell.* New York: Century, 1931. A fascinating look at Bolivia and the Amazon basin in the early twentieth century.

Yossi Ghinsberg, *Back from Tuichi.* New York: Random House, 1993. A chilling look at being lost in the Amazon basin.

Rex A. Hudson, ed., *Bolivia: A Country Study.* Washington, DC: Library of Congress, Federal Research Division, 1991. Very complete background material on all aspects of Bolivia.

Herbert S. Klein, *Bolivia: The Evolution of a Multi-Ethnic Society.* New York: Oxford University Press, 1992. A scholarly study of how Bolivia came to be the nation it is today in terms of economics and politics.

James M. Malloy and Richard S. Thorn, eds., *Beyond the Revolution: Bolivia Since 1952.* Pittsburgh: University of Pittsburgh Press, 1971. Provides scholarly insight into many areas of Bolivia before, during, and since the revolution.

Michael A. Malpass, *Daily Life in the Inca Empire.* Westport, CT: Greenwood Press, 1996. A detailed study of all aspects of Inca life and times.

Magnus Morner, *The Andean Past: Land, Societies, and Conflicts.* New York: Columbia University Press, 1985. Offers a comprehensive history of the area and society that constituted the Inca empire.

Maria Rostworowski de Diez Canseco, *History of the Inca Realm.* New York: Cambridge University Press, 1999. Provides detailed information on the rise, rule, and fall of the Inca realm.

Thomas Rourke, *Man of Glory: Simón Bolívar.* New York: William Morrow, 1939. Provides in-depth information on Bolívar's life, including many of Bolívar's quotes.

Rebecca Stone-Miller, *Art of the Andes: From Chavin to Inca.* New York: Thames and Hudson, 1995. A well-illustrated volume discussing artifacts from 500 B.C. through the time of the Inca.

Deanna Swaney, *Bolivia: A Lonely Planet Travel Survival Kit.* Oakland, CA: Loney Planet Publications, 1996. Full of interesting, detailed, and practical information about Bolivia.

PERIODICALS

Robert Alexander, "Bolivia's Democratic Experiment," *Current History*, February 1985, pp. 76–80.

Tatiana Pina, "Art Student Strives to Preserve the Traditions of His People," *Providence Journal*, May 10, 2001.

Larry Rohter, "Embattled Bolivian Leader Submits Letter of Resignation," *New York Times*, October 18, 2003.

INTERNET SOURCES

Travelvantage, "Bolivia." www.travelvantage.com

INDEX

Picture Credits

About the Author

Marguerite A. Kistler lives in Pittsburgh, Pennsylvania, and has been a teacher for twenty years. She has a bachelor's degree in secondary English education from Cedarville University and a master's degree in reading education from the University of Pittsburgh.